The Interior Design Bo

The Interior Design Book For A Happy Home

Sofia Meri

Published by LAURENT MERI, 2023.

THE INTERIOR DESIGN BOOK FOR A HAPPY HOME

First edition. August 31, 2023.

Written by Sofia Meri.

Table of Contents

Dedicated to all the creative spirits ready to unapologetically decorate homes as vibrant, nostalgic, and emotionally uplifting as their souls

By Sofia Meri

Welcome to the happy home of your dreams! Within these pages, you'll find everything you need to surround yourself with uplifting décor that reflects your unique spirit.

This book is intended as a guide, not a rulebook. It contains tips and principles, not strict steps or required checklists. The goal is simply to help you gain clarity around your own decorating style and confidence in designing feel-good spaces that spark inspiration.

There's no need to read the chapters in order or apply every suggestion exactly as written. Feel free to skip around to the sections most appealing and relevant to your needs. Absorb what resonates, then adapt the concepts in ways that feel authentic to you.

Decorating should be an enjoyable process of self-discovery, not a stressful quest for perfection. Progress will happen organically over time through Trial and error as you learn more about your tastes and what environments lift you up. Give yourself permission to play, experiment and get creative without self-judgment.

You may want to keep this book handy for when you need a quick hit of inspiration before heading to a thrift store or making updates to your home. Refer back to the tips that stood out most and jot down additional ideas in the margins. Mark pages with Post-Its to easily refind beloved passages.

Most importantly, remember that you are the expert on designing happily inspiring spaces for yourself. Use the guidance in this book as a supportive starting point, then bravely build upon it to craft rooms as unique as your spirit. Surround yourself with pieces, colors, and styles that authentically resonate with your energy.

Now, let's begin exploring the principles of uplifting dopamine decor! Wishing you many delightful hours spent creating a cozy, colorful, creativity-sparking haven. May your home become a sacred space shining with the light of your one-of-a-kind essence. Let's do this!

Enhancing Your Reading with Complementary Visuals

While this guide focuses on clearly articulating the philosophies, psychology, and foundational principles behind dopamine decorating through words, I recognize many readers also appreciate accompanying visual examples.

Pictures allow you to vividly envision how these uplifting design concepts might translate into tangible spaces, color palettes, arrangements, and motifs. You conceptualize more fully when absorbing principles both verbally and visually.

That's why I offer access to the Sofia Meri Interior Design Guide. This photo-rich online resource excellently demonstrates visual examples.

With vivid imagery of finished spaces, the duide allows you to illuminated this book in action.

Scan or follow the link below

rebrand.ly/SofiaMeri

Dopamine Decor Interior Design For A Happy Life

Welcome to the happy home of your dreams! With the turn of this page, you're taking the first step towards creating a living space that fully reflects the colorful, playful, and warm vibes of your unique personality. If the sea of sterile, all-white apartments and homes marked by mass-produced decor makes you yearn for something more vibrant and meaningful, you've come to the right place.

In this book, we'll explore the blithe spirit of **dopamine decor** – an interior design approach focused entirely on surrounding yourself with furniture, art, textiles, colors, and treasured keepsakes that spark joy deep within your soul. Unlike fleeting trends that come and go, dopamine decor is forever. Why? Because it's inherently based on you – your distinctive style, favorite aesthetics, and the nostalgic pieces that never fail to make you smile.

While some minimalist homes may boast sleek lines and tidy organization, they often lack the levity and heart that turns a house into a happy home. Through dopamine decorating, we inject lightness and life back into interior design, embracing playful patterns, radiant colors, time-honored family heirlooms, and tactile textures that beg to be touched. This signature style provides the perfect antidote to cookie-cutter rooms devoid of personality.

Within these pages, our goal is to help you curate spaces brimming with joy, energy, and nostalgia. You won't find strict rules here or pressure to conform to fleeting fads. Instead, through a series of fun exercises, prompts, and decor dilemmas, we'll explore your cherished memories, favorite aesthetics, and unique quirks to uncover design choices that authentically represent you.

While creating a beautifully personalized haven, we'll also discuss key principles of color theory, sourcing special finds, displaying memorabilia, and pulling rooms together seamlessly. You can start small with pops of sunny yellow pillows or go all-in by bathed your bedroom in your favorite hue from floor to ceiling. The beauty of dopamine decor is that it meets you wherever you're at in your design journey and grows as you do.

This book was created to help you follow your creative spirit without reservation or limitation. Within these pages, you have the encouragement and guidance needed to transform your home into a playful, energizing oasis where you can recharge and be wholly, authentically you. As you turn each page, remember that there are no rules in dopamine decor – only joy. Any choice that brings you happiness and nostalgic warmth belongs in your space.

Are you ready to immerse yourself in colors that lift your mood, prints that make you smile, and treasured finds filled with memories and meaning? Then let's get started designing your dreamiest, happiest home yet! Permission granted to have fun.

The first step in dopamine decorating is getting clear on your goals, lifestyle needs, budget, and timeline. Rushing into design choices without thoughtful reflection can leave you with a disjointed space that doesn't fully support you. But don't worry – clarifying your vision doesn't have to be laborious. We'll make the process uplifting and enlightening.

Let's begin by closing your eyes and picturing your ideal domestic scene. What do you envision when you imagine a home that makes your heart sing? Cozy reading nooks with pillows and blankets to dive into? A vibrant kitchen where you love whipping up nourishing meals? An oasis of a bedroom bathed in restful hues?

Really let your imagination wander without limitation here. Dream big! Every little detail that crosses your mind, from your ideal color scheme to special pieces of furniture to the very vibe you want to feel when you walk through the door, is an important clue worth noting.

Now, keeping that euphoric vision in mind, let's get down to logistics. Grab a journal or notebook you enjoy writing in and let's capture key practical considerations that will allow your dreamiest domestic vision to manifest in reality.

Start by writing down your overall interior design goals. Do you hope to host cozy dinner parties? Entertain little ones? Maximize natural light? Create zones for work and rest? Get as specific as possible about your aspirations.

Next, make a list of your lifestyle needs and habits. How you actually live day-to-day should take priority in design choices. Note your routines, hobbies, frequently used spaces, and any activities you hope your new interiors will support.

Now, let's talk budget. Be honest here – it's the best way to set yourself up for success. Better to work within your means than end up overspending and overwhelmed. List available funds and financing options. Prioritize must-haves over nice-to-haves.

Finally, record your ideal timeline for completion. Interior design can take time to do thoughtfully. If you want to get settled within a few weeks, we can suggest quick upgrades. More extensive overhauls may take several months from start to finish. Outline expected timing based on your unique constraints.

With your hopes, realities, and limitations clearly spelled out in your trusty notebook, you now have a strong framework in which to start manifesting your happy home vision. We can refer back to these intentions often as we work through design concepts room-by-room in the coming chapters. Whenever you feel unsure or overwhelmed, just glance at your vision prompts to realign with your north star goals.

Time for a quick check-in:

- Do you feel clearer on the overall vibe and function you're going for?

- Got your must-haves and nice-to-haves recorded?

- Feel aligned with your budgetary limits and timing?

- Ready to really immerse in bringing your dreams to life?

If you answered yes, wonderful! Hold onto that clarity and inspiration as we now dive into the heart of dopamine decorating – choosing finishes, furnishings and decorative details tailored to your unique spirit.

Now that you've clarified your vision, let's explore how thoughtful design choices can uplift your spirit and support emotional well-being every single day. Dopamine is the key neurotransmitter that boosts motivation, focus, energy and mood. We'll use science-backed techniques to maximize your daily dose of happy home vibes!

Color is one of the most potent dopamine design tools at your disposal. The hues you choose can shift your outlook and energy level profoundly. Cool tones like blues, greens and purples have tranquil, soothing effects perfect for restful spaces. While warm reds, oranges and yellows energize and uplift the spirit.

Take a moment now to scan your vision journal and make note of any colors that jumped out at you intuitively. Tap into memories of beloved childhood spaces, scenic destinations that gave you joy, even images from dreams. List every hue that resonates as a potential paint color, fabric choice, or accent shade. We'll narrow it down later, but for now, gather all possibilities.

Now, cross-reference your favored hues with common color associations to predict their effects. As you home in on a color palette, consider creating intentional energy zones. For example, invigorating warm tones in the kitchen to start the day motivated. Soothing cooler hues in the bedroom for rest. You might even designate a vivid accent wall somewhere as an instant mood booster!

Beyond paint, infuse color through textiles – pillows, throws, rugs, towels, and linens. Vivid accents against neutral backdrops keep the look cohesive. Display colorful art, ceramics or book collections. Floral decor naturally brings the joy of nature indoors. Just be sure to opt for organic over artificial whenever possible.

Now let's address textures. Tactile elements beg for touch, creating an irresistible sense of coziness. In your dreamy domestic vision, note fabrics you long to cuddle up with. Plush pillows, soft blankets, velvety upholstery, and shag rugs all feed the dopamine decor mission. Balance ultra-smooth and fluffy finishes for maximum sensory delight.

Natural textures enrich a space with organic warmth and character. Play with woven fibers, wooden accents, clay ceramics, marble and stone elements, rattan and wicker furniture. Irregularities and natural variations in tone and pattern bring life to your design.

Lighting sets the mood. Bright, crisp white light energizes and focuses us, perfect for kitchens, offices, and grooming stations. Soft glowing lamps, fairy lights and candles cultivate relaxation before bed. Put lighting on dimmers to adjust the ambience as needed. Near windows? Bring in the joyful brightness of natural daylight whenever possible.

Now, in your decor vision notebook, list any specific pieces you'd love to incorporate – favorite furniture finds, meaningful art, collections to display. Don't limit yourself. We'll edit and refine this wish list together as we design each room. Having guidance from your heart helps ensure dopamine decor choices that spark nostalgia and authentic happiness within your space and soul.

With an understanding of design psychology principles, you're ready to unleash the full joy-sparking potential of your home. In the next chapter, we'll build on this foundation by addressing important structural considerations for optimizing your layout and flow. Get ready to infuse color, texture, lighting and treasured pieces into a beautiful backdrop tailored exactly to you!

Now that we've tapped into vision boards, nostalgic elements, and design psychology, let's address the practical backbone of your space – floorplans and furniture arrangement. This step ensures your happy home functionally supports your lifestyle and rituals.

Start by studying the architectural layout and dimensions of your rooms. Then list how you plan to use each space. For example:

- Living room – Lounging, reading, socializing

- Kitchen – Cooking, casual meals, homework station

- Bedrooms – Sleeping, dressing, meditation zone

- Home office – Work from home, paying bills, planning

Take note of entryways, windows, focal points like fireplaces, and permanent built-ins. Now sketch rough room layouts, mapping traffic flow and placing windows, doors and archways. This spatial awareness helps prevent furniture clashing with home structure.

Use your lifestyle lists to designate activity zones within each room. Areas for conversation, entertainment, dining, study, etc. Then position primary pieces like sofas, beds, and desks accordingly, allowing ample space to move around each.

Related secondary furnishings like side tables, chairs, shelves, and lighting can be positioned later for polishing touches. For now, focus on identifying purposeful zones and arranging key anchors. You can edit and evolve the layouts over time.

Within this structural framework, consider rules of proportion. In living spaces and bedrooms, avoid pushing furnishings against walls on all sides, which feels stiff. Float pieces thoughtfully, allowing traffic flow all around. Leave enough breathing room between pieces and walls.

In dining spaces, make sure room is available to fully seat chairs when pushed out from tables. For desks, allow enough space to push chairs out and avoid feeling confined. Measure furnishings during shopping to ensure ideal fit.

Now, photograph your rough sketches, keeping proportions and spatial flow in mind. This helps visualize arrangements three-dimensionally before acquiring pieces. Use painter's tape to block out scaled layouts right on your floors for further testing.

As we select finishes and decor next, apply the principles of red thread design for pulled-together cohesion room to room. Red thread simply means repeating colors, materials, patterns, or other elements rhythmically throughout your home.

For example, if you adore floral patterns, incorporate flowers prominently in each space. Or if passionate about sage greens and peach tones, use those hues across soft goods and accents to unify rooms. You'll curate a warm, welcoming retreat with dashes of joyful decor that make you smile each time you notice them.

Let's do a layout check-in:

- Did you designate purposeful zones tailored to your needs?

- Do proportions allow space to move and function within rooms?

- Did you map reasonable traffic flow patterns?

- Any red thread aesthetic themes emerging?

With practical floorplans mapped to support your lifestyle, we're ready for the fun part - filling each space with beautiful, dopamine boosting finishes and furnishings!

Today we get to dive into selecting finishes and materials that set the perfect uplifting backdrop for infusing personal belongings and treasured decor. The textures, patterns, and sheens you choose can impart subtle design psychology benefits while also simply sparking joy through their aesthetic appeal. Follow your bliss!

Let's start with flooring. Is gleaming hardwood your dream underfoot? Do colorful tiles or sunny cork call your name? Score style and comfort points by adding plush area rugs overtop base materials. Just be sure to anchor them properly so no one trips. Layered flooring invites the eye downwards to appreciate overlooked beauty.

If laid floors aren't in the budget, no worries! With the right accents and furnishings, even a basic carpet can provide a neutral base for happiness overhead. Remember the power of vertical space.

Speaking of vertical planes, don't underestimate the transformative power of paint. A fresh coat in uplifting hues erases existing drabness. Paint faux treatments like rag rolling, sponging, or stenciling to add artisanal texture. Find removable wallpaper with cheerful patterns forrenter-friendly installations.

Explore sustainably harvested wood panels or tiles as an eco-friendly alternative. Natural grain variations prevent boring uniformity. Mix materials on accent walls - wood with painted drywall, ceramic tile with painted trim, etc. Creative pairings provide visual interest.

For cabinetry, stain finishes in light, mid, or dark wood tones offer a classic look that transitions gracefully over time. The warmth of wood never goes out of style. Or opt for durable paint. Glossy sheens have a tidy, upscale vibe, while velvety matte finishes feel more relaxed.

Tile provides a cheerful, wipeable finish in kitchens and baths. Play with colors, textures, shapes, and patterns. Handmade encaustic tiles offer artisanal beauty. Vintage finds score major dopamine points! Just seal grout religiously.

Where possible, integrate natural stone elements like polished quartz counters or marble accents. These earthy minerals literally ground a space with their cool, solid presence. If mimicking is budget-friendly, go for it. Faux materials have come a long way.

Incorporate metallic finishes sparingly through lighting, hardware, and decor accents. A little glitz goes a long way in most styles. Exceptions include Hollywood glam! Gilded order reigns over tinsel town.

The overarching key is thoughtfulness. Curate an inspiring backdrop that reflects who you are. Your home shouldn't be an afterthought or feels disconnected from your spirit. Make deliberate finish choices that spark creativity and joy.

Let's summarize key material points:

- Layer flooring textures and materials for depth.

- Paint or paper walls in uplifting hues or patterns.

- Choose wood or tile cabinetry for organic warmth.

- Incorporate stone and metallic accents judiciously.

- Select finishes that feel uniquely YOU!

You now have the foundation to build a happy home oasis. Next, we'll dive into curating furniture, textiles and decor that injects cozy, personalized style into your thoughtfully finished spaces!

The furniture, fabrics, and decorative accents you select can make a space sing! While finishes set an uplifting backdrop, these are the fun flourishes that infuse rooms with memories, meaning, and personality. Don't hold back on sourcing special pieces that tell your story.

In each room, identify your focal points – fireplace mantels, reading nooks, desktops, headboards, etc. These areas present primo opportunities to display cherished items imbued with nostalgia. Gather mementos from childhood, vacations, family/friends, hobbies, and milestones.

Curate mini vignettes by pairing a couple meaningful pieces with coordinating decorative objects. For example, mount Grandpa's vintage fishing lures in a shadowbox above a beloved photo of you both. Prop Aunt May's porcelain figurine beside a dried flower from the bouquet at her 50th anniversary party.

For focal shelves and tabletops, gather assorted decorative objects in coordinating colors. Glassware, ceramics, framed photos, coffee table books, candles, bud vases, trays, baskets, and lacquered boxes make classic additions. Rotate trinkets seasonally to keep it fresh.

In choosing furniture, seek out beloved materials like wood, wicker, or metal. Play with fun shapes – curved lines, ovals, circles. These organic silhouettes bring natural elegance. Floral, bird, or animal motifs add whimsical personality.

Upholstery pieces provide plush comfort while allowing you to layer on lively patterns and textures. When uncertain, opt for solids in lighter neutral shades as a base. Then dress with colorful pillows, throws, and armchair cuddlers. Washable slipcovers also reinvent sofas affordably.

Lighting presents another opportunity to amplify joy. Crystal chandeliers, beaded pendants, and curvaceous sconces catch and refract light elegantly. Integrate lampshades in sunny hues or energetic patterns. Set bare bulbs in vintage marquee letters spelling favorite mantras for an uplifting glow.

Your textile choices bring major mood-lifting potential. Source sumptuous bedding, billowy window panels, cozy shag throw rugs, cheerful dish towels, and quirky accent pillows. Natural fibers like cotton, linen and jute feel ultra-inviting.

If opting for a delicate heirloom quilt or handmade weaving, consider encasing it in glass on the wall for preservation. The meaningful stories woven into cherished textiles deserve protection.

This book was created to help you follow your creative spirit without reservation or limitation. Within these pages, you have the encouragement and guidance needed to transform your home into a playful, energizing oasis where you can recharge and be wholly, authentically you. As you turn each page, remember that there are no rules in dopamine decor - only joy. Any choice that brings you happiness and nostalgic warmth belongs in your space.

Are you ready to immerse yourself in colors that lift your mood, prints that make you smile, and treasured finds filled with memories and meaning? Then let's get started designing your dreamiest, happiest home yet! Permission granted to have fun.

A Note Before We Begin...

First, thank you sincerely for reading this book! My goal is to provide value and help you create a home environment that lifts your spirit.

If you find the advice in this guide useful for surrounding yourself with joyful décor, you'd be doing me a massive favor by taking a minute to leave an honest positive review on the platform where you purchased the book. Here's why it matters:

Positive word-of-mouth is crucial for books like this to spread and make an impact. Your review gives algorithms a signal that these dopamine decorating tips are helping people live happier lives.

That then allows me to reach and assist many more design enthusiasts just like you. My dream is improving wellbeing at scale by teaching people how to turn their homes into personal sanctuaries through purposeful décor.

But that can't happen without reviews from awesome readers. And you are an AWE...SOMe reader! So if this book resonates with you, please boost the signal with a positive review. It would mean the world to me and this community.

Shifting home décor habits isn't easy – we need all the inspiration we can get! With your small action, together we can share this uplifting message more widely and spark positive changes.

Plus, you'll likely inspire someone in your life who needs this book too. Paying it forward creates ripples.

Okay, sincerely thank you for even considering leaving your feedback. Now let's dive into these unbelievable décor upgrades!

Chapter 1: Understanding Dopamine Decor

The Meaning and Principles of Dopamine Décor

What exactly is dopamine decor, and how does it differ from fleeting interior design fads? At its core, this style is about creating uplifting spaces that showcase your personality by surrounding yourself with treasured items that evoke happiness. Rather than catering to trends, the primary goal is to design an environment that makes you smile each day.

Unlike minimalism, which promotes sparseness and stark, neutral colors, dopamine décor fully embraces maximalism, color, sentimentality, and above all, fun. While some may call this style busy or over-the-top, that energy is precisely what makes a space distinctly you. Your home should be filled with pieces that tell your story.

The beauty of dopamine decor is that it puts personalized design over perfection. There is no checklist of rules to follow or trendy aesthetics to replicate. Instead, you simply incorporate furniture, art, colors, textures, and accessories that capture your interests, joys, and nostalgic memories. This could mean displaying your favorite books, collecting quirky ceramic creatures, or arranging family photos in colorful frames.

Leave guilt over what's fashionable behind – your space was not created to impress guests or adhere to someone else's style standards. Dopamine decor is all about letting your inner child run freely through each room, embracing the freedom to be playful, eclectic, and even wonderfully weird.

Principles of Dopamine Décor

Now that we understand the "why" behind dopamine decorating, let's explore the "how" by covering key guiding principles:

Focus on feelings. Above all else, every decorative choice should spark positive emotions, whether it's cheerfulness, relaxation, or nostalgia. Select pieces that make your heart sing.

Maximize color. Vibrant, saturated hues energize and uplift us, so use them abundantly through painted walls, fabrics, and accessories. Don't be afraid to go bold.

Layer in texture. Incorporate natural materials like wood and rattan along with soft textiles that beg to be touched, like velvet, corduroy, or cashmere. This adds depth and visual interest.

Display memorabilia. Curate shelves of cherished photos, collectibles, souvenirs, and keepsakes that hold sentimental value and tell your unique story.

Have fun with your space! Dopamine decorating means letting loose and not taking interior design too seriously. Don't be afraid to break design "rules" to create rooms that channel your playful spirit.

Embrace your interests. Showcase your hobbies, passions, and quirks through your design choices. Surround yourself with pieces that authentically reflect who you are.

Start small. You don't have to overhaul your entire home overnight. Test out dopamine decor with little additions like throw pillows, funky wall art, or a bright lampshade.

Mix high and low. Eclectically blending thrift store steals, hand-me-down heirlooms, personalized DIY projects, and splurge-worthy new items creates depth.

Keep organization in mind. While rich visual texture is key, don't let your space become cluttered. Use thoughtful storage to maintain a happy level of tidiness.

The most fundamental takeaway when it comes to designing a dopamine-inducing environment is this: Decorate boldly and unabashedly according to what makes your soul sing, not what's considered stylish or on-trend.

Your home should be distinctly you from the moment you walk through the front door. Surround yourself with pieces that reflect your spirit. Curate your very own feel-good space brimming with positive memories and a captivating visual feast for the senses.

It's time to take yourself off decorating autopilot and channel your inner child once more. Let color, imagination, playfulness, and nostalgia be your guides. Your home is meant to be an uplifting retreat for you alone, not a showroom. Therefore, the only style that matters is the one that brings you genuine happiness and joy every single day.

The Whimsical World of Dopamine Décor

Now that we've covered the core principles of this personalized, nostalgia-driven style, let's dive deeper into the playful spirit and visual aesthetic of dopamine decorating. This style wholeheartedly embraces charmingly cluttered, delightfully quirky interiors that channel childlike wonder.

Leave sterile, sparse, all-white rooms behind. A dopamine decor haven is layered with color, texture, meaningful memorabilia, and unexpected whimsy. You'll discover vignettes of collected oddities like a menagerie of ceramic creatures, rows of vintage books, or displays of colorful glass bottles.

The overall look can appear almost magician's cottage-esque – a cozy, enveloping space that reveals new details wherever the eye lands. A set of hand-painted china tucked in an open-faced cabinet. Frames showcasing delicate botanical prints. A moon phase accent wall.

Every object tells a story. The tarnished silver tea set found in your grandma's attic now gleams proudly on the dining table. While the sea glass and shells gathered during childhood beach vacations fill apothecary jars on the windowsill. Your home reflects where you've been.

In a dopamine decor sanctuary, no color or pattern is off limits! The interior palette skews vibrant, embracing jewel tones, bright pops, energetic neutrals, and playful rainbow-hued accents. You'll find graphic palm leaf or floral wallpapers, rugs boasting Moroccan motifs, and colorfully striped fabrics.

The maximalist layering of richly colored textiles and textures creates depth and visual interest while also cultivating an enveloping sense of coziness. Throw a handknit blanket over the back of a leather club chair. Arrange velvet pillows atop a dining bench. Hang tactile macrame wall art above a rattan bookshelf. The senses come alive.

This signature style also incorporates natural materials like wood, wicker, jute, cotton, linen, and wool which bring organic warmth and comfort into a space. Aged and patinated finishes add nostalgic character – a reclaimed wood coffee table, vintage rug, antiqued metal accents, peeling chippy paint. Imperfections grant charm.

Secret nooks and crannies provide playful spots for discovery. Look behind a corner bookcase to find a window seat blanketed in pillows. Peep beneath the clawed feet of a cabinet to spot a favorite childhood toy. Open a vintage steamer trunk doubling as a side table to uncover stacks of old magazines and notebooks.

Follow your fancy by tucking tiny seasonal vignettes wherever inspiration strikes. A mini fall scene with acorns and maple leaves hidden in an empty drawer. A Valentine's display of roses and chocolates styled in a cabinet. Let your imagination run free!

A home decorated according to dopamine design principles feels like an eclectic cabinet of curiosities where you delight in uncovering new treasures each day. Every choice stems from nostalgia, whimsy, and the freedom to fearlessly embrace your own quirky style.

Permission is granted to be unconventional. To break design "rules" in favor of creating a space that ignites childlike joy and wonder. Aim for rooms that envelop you in playfulness, color, treasured keepsakes, and most importantly, happiness. Your home is your haven, so decorate entirely according to what lifts your spirit.

The Art of Displaying Meaningful Memorabilia

A hallmark of dopamine decorating involves prominently displaying nostalgic mementos, keepsakes, and other items of sentimental value within your space. Surrounding yourself with these beloved memory-imbued pieces daily provides an uplifting emotional boost. But how do you artfully showcase memorabilia without veering into cluttered or chaotic territory? Follow these tips:

Curate thematic vignettes - Gather a few special items that share a common theme or era and arrange them together in a designated display area to tell a nostalgic visual story. For example, childhood vacation souvenirs on a bedroom shelf or dance trophies above your barre in the home studio.

Utilize frames and shadowboxes - Photos, medals, event badges, concert tickets, and other flat ephemera can be framed or displayed in a shadowbox to keep important memorabilia intact and protected under glass.

Incorporate items into practical decor - Cherished hardcover books become decor on shelves. Vintage luggage gets new life as a coffee table base. Your grandma's antique sewing machine serves as a console table. Repurpose meaningful pieces as functional decor.

Label treasures - Use small plaques, framed index cards, or tags attached to string to label antique family items or other ambiguous objects so their history and significance is clear.

Showcase collections - Unify collections like vintage postcards, sea glass, or figurines through attractive coordinated display methods like framed groupings, sets of matching dishes, or coordinated shelving to keep items from appearing jumbled.

Rotate seasonal mementos - To prevent overwhelming clutter, box certain holiday or seasonal memorabilia when not in season for fresh annual rediscovery.

Preserve with care - Heirlooms and fragile items deserve special care. Protect them in enclosed shadowboxes or shelving with glass doors to limit dust and damage over time.

The key to avoiding a cluttered appearance is editing - include only your most cherished items and display them intentionally in an organized, thematic manner. Surround collections and vignettes with enough negative space to prevent visual overload. When curating any space with meaningful memorabilia, quality over quantity remains the guiding principle for creating an uplifting display that sparks nostalgia and joy.

Infusing Personality Through Colorful Accent Walls

Nothing allows you to instantly infuse vibrant personality into a room quite like a brightly colored accent wall. This bold decorative choice provides a powerful yet affordable dopamine boost. When executed thoughtfully, an accent wall enlivens your space and reflects the colorful essence of your spirit.

But how do you choose the perfect vibrant hue? Start by considering the mood you want to cultivate in a particular space. Jewel tones, bright citrus shades, and warm earth tones provide an energizing punch. While soft pastels and cool tones create a more relaxing vibe.

Look for colors connected to positive memories and emotions. The sunny yellow of your childhood bedroom walls. The ocean blue of your favorite beach destination. Select a shade that makes your heart sing.

Next, assess how the color will interact with existing elements in the space like flooring, furniture, and lighting. You want your accent tone to feel cohesive, not clashing. Sample paint strips on walls and move them throughout the day to judge color accuracy.

Incorporate complementary accents like textiles, pillows and artwork that contain notes of your featured color to tie the whole room together beautifully. Too matchy-matchy can feel one-dimensional, so aim for a purposeful eclectic blend.

Paint is the most cost-effective way to create an accent wall, but don't overlook creative alternatives like...

- Wallpaper with cheerful patterns
- Removable wall decals
- Gallery photo collages
- Framed vintage scarves or tapestries
- Fabric installed using liquid starch

The options are endless when selecting a colorful focal feature wall that showcases your personality! An accent wall allows you to take decorating risks while still keeping other walls neutrally flexible.

Most importantly, choose colors and patterns unapologetically based on your own tastes and joys - not what's considered trendy. An accent wall is meant to be a boldly personalized statement. So decorate freely and have fun making your space pop!

Strategically Incorporating Houseplants for Maximum Impact

In addition to color, artwork and textiles, one of the most powerful ways to imbue a space with a feel-good dopamine boost involves strategic use of lively greenery. Thoughtfully incorporated plants cultivate energy, tranquility and a sense of vitality within your home. Follow these tips for maximizing the joy and style payoff of your botanical accents:

Focus on favorite varieties - Opt for plants that hold personal meaning from childhood gardens, are connected to cherished memories, or simply capture your imagination. For example, orchids or air plants for their sculptural uniqueness or herbs for their scent and usefulness.

Consider practical needs - When selecting houseplants, factor in lighting requirements, maintenance needs, watering frequency, and your general plant care aptitude. Choose plants well-suited for your specific growing conditions.

Highlight through design - Use elongated planters, hanging pots, tall shelving, wall mounts, macrame hangers, and plant stands to elevate greenery to eye-level and make it a true decorative focal point.

Curate through coordination - Groupings of plants with coordinated colors and pot styles make more of an impact than scattered singles. Create little vignettes through repetition of planters.

Define style intention - The vibe you want to create will inform what varieties you choose. For bohemian spaces, trailing vines, large tropicals and suspend

How dopamine decor promotes happiness and wellbeing

The Science Behind Dopamine Décor

While the word itself contains "dopamine," the feel-good neurochemical, the happiness-boosting benefits of this decor style are far more than just a namesake. The strategic use of color, meaningful memorabilia, and nostalgic textures fosters positive emotions and improves overall wellbeing. Science shows that our environment directly impacts mood. Therefore, intentionally designing our homes to uplift can make a significant difference in our daily lives.

Color Psychology

The abundant use of vibrant, saturated color is a hallmark of dopamine décor. But color isn't simply added for aesthetics – its selection is science-based. Studies show that different hues directly influence emotions and behaviors. Let's explore how to effectively wield the power of color:

- Yellow - This cheerful hue stimulates the release of serotonin and dopamine, bringing on a boost of happiness and confidence. Use it when you need a pick-me-up.

- Red - Associated with love, intimacy, and strength, red also raises heart rate and captures attention, making it perfect for accent walls or energizing workspace.

- Pink - Tones of pink promote relaxation and diffuse aggression and anxiety. Its gently feminine vibe is ideal for bedrooms.

- Orange - This vibrant, sunny color boosts energy and enhances mood. Use orange accessories and art for an instant dose of delight.

- Green - From mint to emerald, green evokes renewal, harmony, and freshness. Incorporate this color to cultivate peaceful spaces.

- Blue - Cool hues of blue are strongly tied to relaxation and productivity. Paint your office robin's egg blue for a soothing work environment.

- Purple - Traditionally a color of luxury and creativity, purple can awaken imagination. Use it in playrooms or home offices.

We will revisit this concept in the section called "Harnessing the Science of Color Psychology" to explore how to effectively leverage the power of color within your space.

Optimism Boost

Incorporating motivational quotes, affirmation art prints, and inspiring images lifts our spirits, outlook, and self-belief. Displaying meaningful quotes, staying surrounded by positive messaging, and gazing upon uplifting photography infuses our environment with optimism and possibility.

Dopamine décor maximizes this beneficial effect by prominently showcasing inspiring quotes, affirmations, and images within each living space. For example, framing treasured inspiring passages above your workspace to stay motivated or displaying a scenic print that evokes wanderlust and adventure above your sofa.

Start by gathering quotes and affirmations that resonate and reproduce them as decorative art pieces, framed photos, throw pillows or wall decals. Search sites like Etsy for ready-made pieces to quickly incorporate uplifting messaging into your space.

For photography or prints, look for images that symbolize dreams, evoke possibility, showcase natural wonders, or depict people positively overcoming challenges through perseverance. Surrounding yourself daily with visual reminders of human potential and the beauty of nature and life subconsciously shifts perspective away from the negative.

Memory Activation

Dopamine décor leverages nostalgia by incorporating meaningful memorabilia and keepsakes that spark treasured recollections and emotions tied to fond memories. Photos of loved ones, travel souvenirs, vintage family heirlooms, and items from our childhood comfort us and conjure happy reflections.

Display these nostalgic pieces prominently in places you frequent daily like above your desk, on the refrigerator, on bedside tables, or grouped in a shadowbox collage over the sofa.

Do you have old ticket stubs or maps from a backpacking adventure across Europe? Frame them! Tiny stones, acorns or shells from the backyard adventures of childhood? Gather them in a glass apothecary jar!

By keeping these memory triggers in plain sight, your brain forms positive associations between treasured belongings and feel-good recollections. Soon a glimpse of Grandma's china teacup elicits a cascade of comforting reflections. Surround yourself with personal mementos to reap the mood-lifting effects of nostalgia daily.

Mental Restoration

Natural textures and cozy, soft furnishings satisfy our senses and promote deep rest and rejuvenation. Cashmere throws, velvet pillows, sheepskin rugs, live plants, and wooden accents bring natural serenity to inner-city apartments. Interacting with natural materials is mentally restoring.

In today's busy modern world full of technology and screens, making a conscious effort to incorporate natural elements and textures into your living space provides a soothing respite for the senses.

Use natural fibers like cotton, linen, jute and wool when sourcing textiles like blankets, pillows and rugs. Swap out synthetics for wooden furniture, accessories and architectural accents wherever possible. Ensure each room includes living greenery like potted plants, herbs and flowers.

The inherent relaxation benefits of interacting with natural materials lowers stress, anxiety, depression and irritability levels over time, while improving sleep quality and mental clarity. Therefore, infusing one's living space with organic textures is a powerful yet affordable mental health boost.

Imagination Ignition

Whimsy and playfulness nurture creativity and imagination. By embracing your inner child and opting for fun, colorful, handmade, or eccentric décor, you build an environment that ignites original thought and freedom of expression. Your home should fuel your imagination, not restrain it.

Unfortunately, many adults limit their living spaces to boring beiges and minimalist, mass-produced décor in an effort to appear mature, trendy or respectable. But imaginative elements awaken our inner spirit.

Dopamine décor grants you permission to reclaim unabashed playfulness. Display quirky ceramic figurines and carousels of colorful hand-blown glass. Stencil song lyrics or poems onto your bedroom wall. Hang a swing or birdcage chair.

Paint bold geometric murals. Paper mâché giant flowers to mount on your wall. Drape string lights and paper lanterns from the ceiling to create a playful fort effect. Install wall decals of butterflies, hot air balloons or magic wands.

Surround yourself with whimsical pieces that make your heart flutter with childlike wonder and joy. Not only will it lift your mood, but igniting your imagination through playful spaces also boosts creativity, problem-solving and mental agility!

Personality Showcasing

Above all, dopamine décor grants you the courage to authentically showcase your tastes and passion through every design choice. Surrounding yourself with pieces imbued with personal meaning, in colors that resonate with you, displayed in ways that channel your unique personality maximizes enjoyment of your space by creating an inspiring reflection of you.

For far too long, women in particular have been taught to restrain self-expression and dim their light to avoid judgment. But the truth is, boldly declaring your interests and essence through your living environment is profoundly empowering.

Every object, color, print, textile and furniture piece offers an opportunity to broadcast something about who you are. For example, showcase your love of dancing by mounting ballet shoes above your barre. A passion for marine life? Incorporate coral and shell accents. Mid-century modern enthusiast? Furnish with iconic retro silhouettes.

Use dopamine décor as a form of fearless self-expression by curating a space bursting with pieces that authentically reflect your spirit. The full manifestation of your multi-faceted self deserves to shine.

While society may trivialize the impact of interior design on wellbeing, science confirms that our environment profoundly impacts mood, outlook, and behavior. The stimulating yet soothing nature of dopamine décor caters to our psychological needs, acting as an antidepressant that you live within.

Each décor choice either contributes to your daily happiness or detracts from it. Therefore, crafting a personalized haven using colors, objects, and styles that spark nostalgia and joy is among the wisest investments you can make in your mental health and quality of life.

Here are additional ways dopamine décor benefits wellbeing:

- Increased energy and alertness from bright colors

- Reduced anxiety and depression through preferred aesthetics

- Deepened relaxation response from natural textures

- Strengthened connections between memories and emotions

- Boosted creative output in whimsical spaces

- Strengthened sense of identity from self-expression

In short, surrounding yourself with pieces imbued with personal significance, in colors and patterns that bring you delight positively impacts both psyche and emotional outlook. Dopamine décor leverages the mind-body connection between décor and wellbeing to maximize enjoyment of your living space and life overall.

Harnessing the Science of Color Psychology deep dive

As evidenced already, color selection represents a science-backed way to consciously influence mood, mindset and behavior through interior design. Now let's explore specific color associations and practical applications in further detail. Follow these tips to effectively harness the psychology of color within your home building on what we explained before:

Red

- This bold, passionate hue accelerates pulse and raises blood pressure. It captures attention while also stimulating appetite.

- Use it: In dining spaces to encourage eating. In bedrooms to ignite romance. On accent walls when you need quick energy.

Orange

- Cheery shades of orange evoke sunshine, promoting happiness and warmth. Orange boosts enthusiasm and stimulates mental activity.

- Use it: In living rooms and family spaces to inspire togetherness. In entryways to make first impressions welcoming.

Yellow

- Bright, joyful yellow activates memory and triggers the release of serotonin and dopamine. It boosts mood and livens the spirit.

- Use it: In workspaces to spark creativity. In kitchens to energize each morning. In bedrooms to cultivate optimism.

Green

- From mossy to mint, green tones are mentally stabilizing and physically calming. This restorative color relieves anxiety, irritation and sadness.

- Use it: In bathrooms and bedrooms to relax before sleep. In living rooms to unwind after work. On walls when you feel overwhelmed.

Blue

- Cooler blue tones lower pulse rate and body temperature, aiding concentration. Light blues feel ethereal while navy tones feel grounded.

- Use it: In offices to stay focused. In bathrooms for a soothing spa vibe. In bedrooms to ease insomnia.

Purple

- Traditionally associated with luxury, spirituality and creativity, purple offers a mood-lifting escape. It emboldens imagination and soothes unease.

- Use it: In meditation spaces to foster relaxation and inner peace. In kids' rooms to stir imagination. In bathrooms for a pampering vibe.

Pink

- Feminine pink promotes affection, kindness and hope. Gentler hues have a calming, restorative effect. Bolder pinks feel playful.

- Use it: In bedrooms as a soothing sleep surround. In living areas to soften a space. On walls when you need a comforting hug.

While trends may push you to default to safe neutrals, purposefully wielding the science-backed power of color allows you to actively influence mood, productivity, relaxation and creativity within your home.

Curating a Personalized Gallery Wall

Gallery walls provide the perfect opportunity to boldly infuse personality by bringing together a curated collage of meaningful photos, art and other ephemera. Here's how to thoughtfully compose an uplifting and cohesive gallery display:

Select a wall with ample space for your collection to grow. Position furniture first to determine ideal placement. Measure the wall area to calculate rough frame spacing.

Gather cherished photos and art. Look for varied orientations, colors and sizes to add interest. Photos grouped by theme or color palette achieve a neat editorial effect.

Incorporate special items beyond just frames, like pressed flowers or leaves, string lights, wall decals, colorful ribbons, handwritten notes or old event tickets pinned by thumbtacks. These personalized layers add charm.

Play with arrangement and spacing until pleasing to the eye. Build visual triangles by clustering 3-4 items together in sections across the larger display. Keep similar framing and mat colors.

Hang frames at slightly different heights for a dynamic look, but keep the bottom edges somewhat aligned for polish. Use removable mounting putty to experiment until spacing feels right.

Edit periodically as your collection evolves. Add new meaningful mementos. Remove clutter. Reconfigure items into new pleasing patterns. Gallery walls document cherished memories.

Approach curating your gallery wall as an ongoing DIY scrapbooking activity. Over time it organically evolves into an uplifting reflection of people, places and passions most meaningful to you.

The key is thoughtfully incorporating photos, art, and ephemera that capture nostalgic memories and reflect your unique personality. Let this prominent display stir joy and inspiration each time your eyes land on a cherished image.

Strategic Incorporation of Houseplants

In addition to color, texture and meaningful memorabilia, living plants infuse spaces with revitalizing energy and life. When strategically incorporated, greenery elevates style and wellbeing. Follow these tips for maximizing the joy and visual impact of plants in your home:

Seek out varieties you feel drawn to - There are endless options when selecting houseplants. Lean into what resonates by choosing plants you feel intuitively connected to through scent, appearance or meaning.

Play with heights and shapes - Incorporate a mix of trailing, cascading, tall, bushy, wide and narrow plants. Varying silhouettes create more dynamic arrangements.

Use planters to elevate and highlight - Opt for ceramic pots with visually weighty bases for stability. Pole planters, hanging pots, wall mounted displays or multi-tiered plant stands showcase greenery at eye-level.

Create groupings and vignettes - Style plants in purposeful clusters of 3-5 coordinating pots. Repeating planter colors or textures achieves a cohesive botanical display.

Consider air purifying and pet-friendly varieties - Plants like aloe, peace lilies, spider plants, snake plants and philodendrons filter indoor air. Some even deter pet toxicity when nibbled.

Add grow lights where needed - Supplement natural light with adjustable full spectrum grow bulbs. Timer settings automate proper lighting duration for thriving plants.

Greenery brings vitality, freshness and a mood-lifting energy infusion to interior spaces. Allow favorite plants to take decor prominence through strategic placement and coordinating pots. Surrounding ourselves with abundant plants cultivates our own growth and renewal from within. Soon your home feels like a nurturing greenhouse, sheltering your dreams as you progress toward fruition.

The Design Elements That Define Dopamine Décor: color, texture, memorabilia

What are the integral ingredients that comprise this uplifting style? Dopamine decor ultimately comes down to the strategic use of vivid color, natural texture, and nostalgic memorabilia. When used in harmony, these three design elements create living spaces that boost mood, inspire imagination, and promote authentic self-expression.

The Power of Vibrant Color

Color is arguably the quintessential visual component of dopamine décor. Rich, saturated hues applied through paint, fabric, furniture, and art inject vibrant energy into any space. The strategic use of color is what primarily sets this style apart from muted, minimalist décor.

Why is color so integral to dopamine design? Pigment has an innate ability to alter human perception, emotion, and behavior. An influx of lively hues instantly lifts one's mood. Here are specific ways to effectively incorporate color:

● Paint your walls an energetic hue like coral, mint, or yellow - Colorful walls establish an uplifting backdrop.

● Choose colorful furniture & accessories - Vibrant pillows, art, rugs, and décor enliven a room.

● Use multiple complementary colors - Pair shades like blue and orange or pink and green.

● Establish a color palette - Stick to 3-5 core hues for cohesion.

● Add pops of brightness - Use citrine and turquoise in doses for punctuation.

● Incorporate color blocked patterns - Bold geometric and graphic prints add visual dynamism.

● Experiment with different saturations - Mix muted and maxed-out shades.

● Keep the colors personal - Select hues linked to positive memories.

Remember, dopamine décor is about surround yourself with colors that make you happy, not selecting hues simply because they are deemed "in." Lean into colors that hold personal meaning or remind you of beloved places and people.

The Warmth of Natural Texture

In addition to vibrant color, an abundance of natural textures is integral for creating that cozy, nostalgic atmosphere synonymous with dopamine design. Tactile layers lend a sense of depth, comfort, and inviting softness.

Natural woven fibers like jute, seagrass, cotton, and bamboo add casual texture. Cashmere, fleece, velvet, and chenille offer plush softness. Wood finishes, ceramic accents, and woven rattan contribute organic texture. Macramé wall hangings provide pure tactile intrigue.

When sourcing natural texture, prioritize pieces that seem pleasing to touch. Seek out furnishings and accents that just beg to be handled. We inherently crave touching inviting textures. Channel this draw by peppering in slubby throws, ceramic lamps, rattan poufs, and wooden bowls.

Here are more ways to effectively incorporate natural texture:

- Layer in woven blankets and shag pillows
- Select furniture with textural fabric like bouclé, terry cloth, or tweed
- Bring the outdoors in with ceramic planters and vases
- Incorporate wood elements like bowls, trays, and wall panels
- Display organic pieces like driftwood, stones, and shells
- Hang textural wall tapestries and macramé art
- Use nubby jute, seagrass, hemp rugs and baskets
- Accent with wicker, rattan, raffia and bamboo
- Add wool knits like throw blankets and pillows
- Showcase collections of natural objects

Texture connects us to our primal roots through touch. Selecting natural finishes satisfies our senses while bringing organic depth into modern spaces. Layer in these tactile elements to create a comforting, artisanal haven.

The Nostalgia of Cherished Memorabilia

The final element that defines dopamine decorating is the prominent display of nostalgic memorabilia. These sentimental items spark treasured memories and comfort us through their emotional associations.

Meaningful memorabilia you can creatively incorporate includes:

- Family photos - Frame special moments and relatives.

- Souvenirs - Display pieces that remind you of adventures.

- Collections - Exhibit any sets of objects you've gathered.

- Antiques - Upcycle your grandparents' furnishings.

- Albums - Showcase cherished records or stickers.

- Artifacts - Highlight items linked to hobbies and passions.

- Posters - Hang onto old artwork and prints.

- Childhood objects - Keep toys, books, or clothing for decoration.

The cherished memorabilia you choose to put on display should have a personal significance based on your own memories and life experiences. These special pieces imbue our homes with nostalgic emotion.

Here are tips for effectively showcasing mementos:

- Designate display areas like mantels or shelves to exhibit meaningful objects in grouped vignettes.

- Frame cherished photos, badges, ribbons, postcards or maps to preserve and protect.

- Incorporate memorabilia into practical décor like using antique furniture pieces.

- Add labels to identify ambiguous artifacts and convey their history.

- Rotate themed collections seasonally for fresh rediscovery.

- Use enclosed shadowboxes to protect fragile heirlooms from dust and light damage.

- Gather like items into thematic mosaic collages for cohesive displays.

Your personally meaningful possessions deserve to be prominently displayed rather than tucked away in boxes. Surround yourself with nostalgic treasures that tell your unique story.

The Interplay of Elements

Used individually, color, texture and memorabilia greatly enhance a space. But incorporated together harmoniously, they take on a transformative power - jointly creating vibrant, multilayered interiors rich with emotion, meaning and sensory delight.

You may choose a nostalgic seafoam green wall color, then build on that peaceful shade by layering in natural jute rugs, cotton throws, wood furnishings, and favorite beach mementos.

Or develop a signature palette of blush pink, mustard and emerald green, then accent with velvet pillows, rattan chairs, and childhood photos in matching frames.

When the three elements unite, the style alchemy is complete - rooms blossom into personalized havens full of heart. Aim for creative interplay between color, texture and memorabilia. Thoughtfully combine all three to fully manifest the spirit of dopamine design in your own uplifting space.

In summary, dopamine décor distinguishes itself from other styles through its unapologetic use of energizing pigment, touchable natural textures, and emotion-evoking keepsakes. When used in harmony, these three elements allow you to create personalized spaces that uplift the spirit, promote wellbeing, and celebrate what makes you undeniably you.

Chapter 2: Defining Your Decor Style

Channeling Your Inner Child

As adults, we often lose touch with the freedom of self-expression and whimsy we once embodied as children. Professional, social, and cultural pressures lead us to abandon beloved aesthetics, interests, and quirks in the name of looking "mature" or "refined." But dopamine decor seeks to turn back the clock – to reconnect with the unrestrained creativity and personality of childhood that gets buried beneath the stresses of adulthood.

Your home should be a safe haven where you make zero apologies for who you are. Through your design choices, find inspiration by revisiting your younger self. Fill your space with pieces that channel the spirit of your childhood. Surround yourself with colors, patterns, textures, and objects reminiscent of joyful and nostalgic times gone by.

To connect with your childhood tastes, ask yourself:

What were my favorite colors as a kid?

- Did I obsess over rainbow hues or gravitate toward pastels? Reintroduce a beloved color palette.

What aesthetic did my childhood bedroom embody?

- Whether it was princess pink or sporty stripes, draw decor inspiration from the rooms you loved most.

Which cartoons, movies, and characters did I adore?

- Display posters, figurines, or prints showcasing beloved pop culture icons and fictional worlds from your youth.

What was my favorite toy or childhood hobby?

- Showcase meaningful items that represent your childhood passions, from Barbies to ballet shoes.

What objects bring on nostalgia?

• Surround yourself with items that prompt fond memories of your upbringing like vintage lunchboxes or boomboxes.

What inspired my imagination as a child?

• Add whimsical pieces that recapture youthful wonder like hanging chairs, hammocks, or canopy beds.

Which emotions did my childhood home fill me with?

• Choose colors and accessories that recreate feelings like joy, tranquility, excitement, or love derived from your upbringing.

While some dismiss childhood preferences as unsophisticated, dopamine décor champions unabashed self-expression. Your tastes need not remain static – they can grow and evolve with you. But first, look inward and find inspiration from the favorite colors, clothes, music, books, games, and aesthetics that set your soul alight as a child.

Many abandon treasured pieces of themselves in the quest to look more polished or refined. But surrounding yourself with pieces imbued with childlike joy and wonder keeps your spirit vibrant and your inner child alive. With your home as a safe haven, give yourself full permission to be playful, have fun, and never fully "grow up."

Here are additional ways to infuse your space with childhood whimsy:

• Display favorite childhood photos and carved initial crafts

• Frame beloved cartoon or storybook art

• Incorporate colors from crayons and markers you loved

• Hang a swing, hammock, or treehouse plywood

• Showcase favorite childhood books and movie memorabilia

• Reintroduce beloved patterns like polka dots or Toile de Jouy

• Mix in furniture from your childhood home

• Hang musical instruments you learned to play as a kid

- Exhibit trophies, medals, and awards from childhood achievements

The beauty of dopamine décor is that it encourages you to proudly showcase pieces of your inner child within your design scheme, not hide them away. Your home should spark creativity, not restrain it. Immerse yourself in aesthetics and interests central to your very identity – ones formed during your wonder years.

Reawakening Your Inner Child

Childhood is a period of innocence, imagination, and authentic self-expression, before the scrutiny and judgment of others leads us to sensor ourselves. But the favorite colors, activities, fictional worlds, and playful perspectives central to our child-selves remain within, ready to be reawakened.

The quest to design a 'mature' space often means rejecting anything 'childish.' But in the safety of your own happy home, give yourself full permission to reconnect with youthful colors, patterns, interests, and nostalgia through your design choices.

Follow your childlike spirit by...

- Choosing a vibrant wall color straight from the crayon box: azure, magenta, canary, violet.

- Dressing in vibrant hues and beloved prints: polka dots, Toile de Jouy, candy stripes, florals.

- Filling your space with memorabilia: framed crayon drawings, snow globes, comic prints, dolls.

- Indulging your inner princess: canopy beds, glittering accents, jewel tones, ruffles.

- Embracing cartoon characters: Hello Kitty dishes, Mickey Mouse posters, superhero prints.

- Displaying awards/trophies: Spelling bee, soccer, gymnastics, karate, ballet.

- Exhibiting collections: Stickers, marbles, rocks, coins, comic books, stamps.

- Showcasing performing arts passions: hang instruments, stage costumes, recital videos.

- Reveling in fantasy & magic: Hogwarts house pride, crystal balls, dream catchers, wands.

Your interests need not remain static. But don't abandon the pieces of yourself that stir nostalgia for the sake of meeting someone else's maturity standards. Through dopamine décor, you can integrate childhood favorites into adult spaces seamlessly.

Many pressures threaten the sacred inner child that resides within us all, but we must protect that fragile creative spirit from losing its luster under layers of external 'shoulds.' Your home décor offers a powerful platform for this self-acceptance. Unapologetically infuse your space with pieces that reconnect you to your youthful essence.

Defining Your Youthful Design Aesthetic

Dopamine decor guiding principles may be universal, but each person's youthful interests, favorite aesthetics, and nostalgic pieces are incredibly personal. Your child-self likely gravitated to particular colors, patterns, themes, fictional worlds, and interests. Capture this individual perspective through décor that lovingly reflects the distinctive hues, objects, and eras central to your upbringing.

To hone in on your unique youthful design aesthetic, reflect on the key formative preferences that shaped your childhood perspective:

- Favorite Colors - Were you drawn to neon hues, pastels, jewel tones, black & white, metallics or earth tones? Incorporate these core colors abundantly.

- Beloved Characters - Did you adore Hello Kitty, Mickey Mouse, superheroes or princesses? Showcase them through prints, figurines and posters.

- Key Eras - Do the 70s, 80s or 90s hold particular nostalgia? Use posters, albums, toys, or clothing to celebrate.

- Personality Traits - Were you bubbly, artsy, athletic or academic? Choose pieces reflecting passions like gymnastics, band, drama or student council.

- Defining Youth Spaces - What did your childhood bedroom or playroom look and feel like? Recreate elements like favorite duvet prints, posters, or furniture pieces.

- Positive Memories - What happy childhood moments can you represent through visuals? Frame family photos from trips to grandma's or days at the county fair.

Youth was a period of self-discovery so aesthetics were incredibly personal, reflective of our budding identity. Surround yourself by pieces that celebrate the indelible essence formed during your early, formative years. Lean into the specific colors, characters, eras, and interests special to you.

For example, as a child of the 80s who loved pandas, pink, and pop music, I might decorate with:

- A bright pink color palette

- Posters of 80s pop icons like Cyndi Lauper

- Baba panda bear figures and accents

- A boombox and cassettes on display

- A pink canopied bed fit for my inner princess

Make youthful nostalgia the inspiration for every decorative choice. Dopamine decor is about fearlessly declaring interests central to your identity through proud displays of associated memorabilia.

Thoughtful Youth Memory Curation

As you identify nostalgic pieces that represent cherished moments and milestones from your wonder years, avoid haphazard, overwhelming displays. Thoughtfully curate vignettes and arrangements that artfully showcase mementos for meaningful impact.

For example, to highlight 1980s childhood memories, I would:

- Gather favorite 80s toys in a glass cabinet to prevent damage.

- Frame striking 80s pop culture magazine ads in coordinating colors.

- Display vinyl records on wall ledges, captioned with artist and year.

- Group sweet photos from childhood trips to grandma's cozy cabin.

- Arrange favorite 80s books on a shelf against a groovy 80s print wallpaper backdrop.

- Fill a bowl with vintage caboodle makeup and accessories for an 80s dress-up corner.

Aim for purposeful displays tied to a particular memory or milestone, not just random scatterings of items. Use frames, risers, shelves, and shadowboxes to thoughtfully showcase, elevate, and protect precious memorabilia.

For extra polish, adhere to principles like:

- Color coordination between frames, prints, book covers.

- Corresponding sizes and shapes.

- Style cohesion between prints, figurines, toys.

- Meaningful labels identifying eras, vacations, relatives.

- Titles and captions to explain ambiguous objects.

Thoughtful curation transforms youth memorabilia from clutter into engaging vignettes brimming with meaning. Take time to artfully arrange nostalgic pieces to prompt a flood of happy recollections as you move through your space.

Conveying Personal History Through Design

Your home tells the story of your life's journey – the places you've been, passions you've pursued, memories made. Therefore, décor should function as visual memoir, showing guests your backstory at a glance. When entering your space, what tale do you want your belongings to collectively tell?

Many default to generic, impersonal decor that reveals little. But you can thoughtfully shape your personal narrative through displayed objects. For example:

- A seashell wreath implies a coastal upbringing.

- Framed photos series shows college friends at a cherished alma mater.

- Antique family furniture passed down from grandparents.

- Trophies from athletic achievements decorate the office.

- Instruments represent music passions pursued over decades.

- Vintage yearbooks sit alongside childhood toy keepsakes.

Groupings should convey a broad life narrative across chapters like childhood, young adulthood, milestones, travels. But also highlight your consistent core identity and passions.

When curating visual vignettes:

- Gather themed items into coordinated displays.

- Use frames, shelves, and cases to show groupings.

- Add era and location details through dates, captions, maps.

- Convey important relationships through family photos.

- Rotate seasonal displays like holiday cards or ornaments.

With thoughtful vignettes and displays, your home becomes a visual memoir recounting life's precious memories and milestones. Surrounding yourself with nostalgic ephemera keeps the past vibrantly alive while bringing deeper meaning to the present.

Preserving Cherished Memorabilia

As you gather sentimental childhood mementos, delicate heirlooms, and paper ephemera to display, preservation is key. Fragile items require protection from sun damage, tearing, or fading over time. Here are tips to safely showcase cherished memorabilia:

- Seal items under UV filtered glass using shadowboxes and frames to encase objects while still showing them off.

- Scan or take quality photos of fragile paper documents like awards or cherished artwork to reprint/frame copies for display while storing originals safely in an album or box.

- For items you wish to touch and interact with, make replicas. For example, scan an old children's book to reprint a fresh copy you can read while keeping the original pristine.

- Use archival plastic photo sleeves, acid-free tissue and cardboard photo boxes to store vintage photos to prevent damage over time. Keep extras not displayed protected.

- Scan old media like cassettes, photo negatives, slides or VHS tapes as digital files you can access from a modern device while preserving outdated original formats.

● Back up digital files, photos, music in multiple places like drives, discs, cloud. Technology changes but your memories should persist.

● Repurpose items in need of retirement like old trophies or artwork into new displays like a shadowbox collage or wall mural where you can still enjoy their sentimental value.

While tempting to freely handle cherished memorabilia, take measures to preserve items whose delicate or outdated nature makes them prone to damage over time. Find ways to retain accessibility to precious mementos while also actively protecting them.

Turning Childhood Fun into Playful Décor

The trappings of adult responsibility threaten our carefree childhood spirit of imagination, play, and sense of wonder. But it's never too late to reawaken the inner child who still resides within. Use purposeful design choices to infuse playfulness and levity into your grown-up space.

For example:

● Designate a whimsical reading nook with plush pillows, fairy lights, and children's books to get lost in.

● Use wall decals and vibrant paint to create a fantasy forest mural straight out of a storybook.

● Add a DIY ball pit, pillowfort, or indoor playhouse area to get silly in.

● Display favorite childhood toys like Lego sets, model train villages, or Barbie Dreamhouses you can still play with.

● Create a dress-up corner with costumes, accessories, jewelry, and hats to spark pretend play.

● Hang a swing, trapeze bar, or treehouse ladder to climb and play on.

● Use chalkboard paint on walls to doodle, write, and draw endlessly.

Don't underestimate the power of play. Allowing your inner child to release through games, imagination, and untamed silliness reduces stress and anxiety levels while keeping your spirit vibrant and perspective uplifted.

Lighthearted touches like plush rugs perfect for lounging with stuffed animals, twinkly string lights overhead, puzzles and games tucked on the shelves turn the everyday act of relaxing at home into a nostalgic childhood wonderland.

Through playful interiors, carefree living is once again at your fingertips.

Honoring nostalgia and sentimental pieces

An integral facet of dopamine decor is prominently displaying nostalgic items that hold sentimental significance in your life story. The memorabilia you choose to exhibit honors heartwarming memories, pays tribute to beloved relationships, and represents treasured aspects of your identity.

Unlike mass produced décor that lacks meaning, your sentimental keepsakes have been lovingly collected over years. They prompt a flood of fond recollections and powerful emotions each time you look upon them. When artfully arranged, these cherished relics bring deeper personalization and heart to your home.

Forms of Sentimental Décor

Sentimental décor can take many forms:

- Photographs - Frame nostalgic moments with family, friends, pets.

- Souvenirs - Display memorable trips and adventures.

- Trophies - Exhibit academic, athletic, career achievements.

- Collections - Showcase any sets of objects you've gathered.

- Antiques - Upcycle relatives' furniture or wedding china.

- Art - Hang onto paintings, pottery, or quilts gifted by loved ones.

- Jewelry - Display cases allow you to highlight special pieces.

- Ticket Stubs - Highlight memorable concerts, games, shows.

- Posters - Hold onto old artwork and prints that still resonate.

- Textiles - Repurpose childhood clothing or blankets.

- Plants - Keep living mementos propagated from relatives' gardens.

- Books - Showcase editions passed down through generations

- Music - Frame iconic records, album art, or concert tees.

By creatively incorporating nostalgic relics, you deepen the meaning and sentimentality of your space. Take time relishing the memories each piece evokes. Let them transport you to times, places, and relationships locked fondly in your heart. Use these sentimental accents as jumping off points for storytelling and reminiscing.

To prevent your home from feeling cluttered, thoughtfully edit your memorabilia collection and keep only pieces that hold special significance. Arrange displays in aesthetic vignettes, not haphazard piles. Lead with cherished photos and sprinkle in complementary accessories. This balances sentimentality with intent and refinement.

Your personal treasures need not be confined to private spaces out of guests' view. Tastefully worked into your décor, they become touchpoints for meaningful connections and charming story swapping. After all, surrounding ourselves with relics imbued with memory helps us celebrate our histories and very identities.

While minimalists may argue sentimental items create visual clutter, dopamine décor proves our keepsakes in fact infuse our homes with nostalgic emotion, personalization, and soul. Life is not meant to be decluttered - it is meant to be cherished. So honor each memento for the love and laughter it represents. Let your home proudly showcase the souvenirs of a life lived vibrantly.

The Power of Personal Photos

Of all sentimental décor, photographs hold special importance for their ability to honor loved ones, capture meaningful milestones, and prompt vivid memories and emotions. Strategically showcasing cherished photos allows you to celebrate relationships, achievements, and adventures that shaped your story.

Here are tips for photo display:

- Frame nostalgic moments with friends, family, children, pets, or partners through the years.

- Create a gallery wall with a collage of meaningful memories and family portraits.

- Display vacation photos that ignite wanderlust or showcase beloved destinations.

- Sprinkle in candid snaps that capture personality and spontaneity.

- Print smartphone photos taken at recent joyful get-togethers and outings for up-to-date memory pops.

- Label extended family images, old childhood photos, or ambiguous moments so their significance is clear.

- Pair prints with related memorabilia like souvenir ticket stubs or event programs.

Photographs freeze precious memories in time, allowing us to vividly relive them through visual triggers. They also celebrate our connections, reminding us of beloved people no longer present in our daily lives. Purposefully displaying nostalgic images immerses you in positive emotions and keeps loved ones symbolically near.

Curating Meaningful Memorabilia Vignettes

While individual sentimental items hold significance, thoughtfully curating vignettes and arrangements amplifies their nostalgic impact. The whole transcends the sum of its parts when objects are displayed in purposeful groupings.

For example:

- On your travel memorabilia shelf, gather souvenirs, photos, maps, even airline tickets and itineraries from a particular cherished trip.

- Style your wedding china, silverware, goblets, and linens together in a cohesive display that represents family heritage.

- Arrange children's books, toys, and photos from your childhood together in a playful memory nook.

Take time playing with arrangements, stepping back to ensure the collection looks polished. The most meaningful displays are thoughtfully composed. Avoid simply scattering random mementos.

Helpful strategies include:

- Choosing coordinating frames, colors, or materials to visually unify items.

- Selecting a specific theme like a beloved family vacation or era in time like the 1980s.

- Layering framed photos with thematic three-dimensional objects.

- Labeling items whose history may be unclear to others.

- Elevating fragile items with risers, stands, or wall mounts.

- Rotating seasonal displays like holiday cards or ornaments.

Aim for sentimental vignettes that thoughtfully honor treasured memories, relationships, places, interests, or times in your life. These displays should spark nostalgia while remaining aesthetically pleasing and cohesive.

Preserving Cherished Memorabilia

When incorporating sentimental memorabilia into your décor, take measures to protect fragile, damaged, or light-sensitive items prone to deterioration over time. Ensure your precious relics persist for years to come through these preservation tips:

- Scan, photocopy, or professionally reprint delicate paperwork to display copies rather than fragile originals.

- Digitize outdated media like records, slides, or VHS tapes while storing originals in archival boxes.

- Seal especially fragile paper documents like letters or certificates inside mats and frames to prevent further damage through handling.

- Repurpose damaged items like old quilts, books or artwork into new displays like pillow covers or wall art so you can continue enjoying their nostalgic charm.

- Use museum glass when custom framing delicate items to protect from UV damage. Request acid-free matting as well.

- Purchase archival plastic sleeves and acid-free tissue to interleave between vintage photos. Store them upright in photo storage boxes.

- Back up digital scans, photos, and home videos in multiple places like external drives, discs, or cloud servers to prevent loss.

While tempting to freely handle precious objects, take measures to preserve their fragile nature where possible. Find creative ways to retain their accessibility while also actively protecting items prone to light, moisture, or tear damage over time. Balance preservation with enjoyment.

Strategic Sentimental Display Areas

Some spaces lend themselves better to sentimental décor than others. Consider prominence, visibility, and traffic flow as you designate special spots for nostalgic curation:

Entryway:

- Framed family photos atop console table

- Meaningful pieces inside glass cabinetry

- Memory ledges to hold cherished objects

- Gallery wall showcasing visual memories

Bedroom:

- Bedside table displays: photos, souvenirs

- Shelves: collections, books, trophies

- Above bed: meaningful artwork/textiles

- Family tree or pin board over desk

Living Room:

- Photo collage wall behind sofa

- Side tables: framed photos, cherished books

- Shelving: collections, souvenirs, antiques

- Fireplace mantel or shelf for vignettes

Home Office:

- Gallery wall: travel prints, photos, maps

- Bookcase: collections, yearbooks, albums

- Desktop: family photos, memorabilia

- Pin board: ticket stubs, postcards

Some displays work best outside of high traffic zones, while entryways and living spaces tend to be ideal for prominent, visible arrangements that cue nostalgia from the moment one enters a home. Feel free to scatter meaningful ephemera anywhere your eye falls, but also designate special memory-centered display areas.

Thoughtfully surrounding yourself with cherished relics allows you to appreciate the treasures of the past, ground yourself in fond memories, and move forward in gratitude - the perfect mindset for a happy home.

The Wellness Benefits of Nostalgic Décor

It's no coincidence that surrounding ourselves with sentimental items linked to joyful memories comforts and uplifts us. Psychology confirms nostalgia provides incredible emotional benefits that support wellbeing.

Specifically, nostalgic reflection:

- Boosts mood and increases happiness by sparking fond recollections

- Elevates self-esteem by reminding us of past accomplishments

- Strengthens social bonds and feelings of love by spotlighting relationships

- Reduces anxiety, stress, and depression by eliciting comforting reflections

- Adds meaning to life by linking the past beautifully with the present

- Fosters optimism and motivation to carry positive memories forward

We all have periods of sadness, loneliness, or frustration. But nostalgic mementos act as an emotional salve, flooding us with warm memories and strengthening our sense of identity. They represent the people, passions, and pursuits that have shaped us.

This is precisely why dopamine decor places such importance on displaying these positive memory triggers. Surrounding yourself daily with nostalgic keepsakes sustains an uplifting sense of connection, achievement, meaning, and possibility even during difficult times.

While decluttering proponents often urge purging sentimental belongings, the psychological benefits of nostalgic reflection prove treasured items do far more good than harm. Use your space to thoughtfully honor your memories.

Making Peace With Imperfect Décor

For many, fear of judgment keeps sentimental items confined to more private spaces instead of proudly on display. But the beauty of dopamine decor is fully embracing the nostalgic and handmade over seeking interior perfection.

You needn't hide cherished items until you somehow replace them with pristine store-bought alternatives. Celebrate their patina of age, handmade charm, or quirky uniqueness.

Your hand-carved camp art project may be amateurish, but its sentimental value outweighs amateur execution. The misshapen vase from your child's art class makes your heart flutter more than polished porcelain ever could.

Much of our hesitance to display precious memorabilia comes down to anxiety over how guests may react to our unconventional style. But surrounding yourself with pieces imbued with history and heart has profoundly positive emotional effects, so why hide it away?

Your loved ones already know and appreciate your backstory, quirks, and nostalgic proclivities. Welcoming guests into spaces showcasing your memorabilia offers intimate insight into your worldview and inner life.

We often think slightly cluttered, eclectic, sentimental style appears unrefined on the surface. But in reality it represents unfiltered self-acceptance and celebration of personal history. There's beauty in that rawness.

Dopamine décor isn't about interior design perfection - it's about boldly declaring through your space: "This is me, past and present". Curate your home as a visual keepsake itself, not a museum. Sentimentality adds soul.

The Evolving Nature of Sentimental Displays

Maintaining an inviting yet memorabilia-filled space requires periodically refreshing displays. Storage solutions keep overflow manageable while rotating items sparks renewed appreciation.

Make nostalgia rotation a rewarding ritual! Each season, switch out cherished decor you've tired of for sentimental pieces long tucked away. Rediscover forgotten gems to redisplay.

Alternatively, evolve certain displays gradually over months or years to highlight new chapters and milestones. For example, expanding a couple's wedding photo display into a relationship timeline capturing dating, homebuying, travels, pregnancies, etc.

Aim to strike a balance by keeping especially meaningful lifelong memorabilia anchors in place while rotating in seasonal accents, fresh photos, recent souvenirs, and newly unearthed vintage gems.

Editing cherished collections also prevents clutter. If your stacks of kids' art overfloweth, regularly cull works to exhibit on a rotating basis. Display only most special trophies or souvenirs while packing the rest.

Maintaining tidy nostalgia requires periodically refreshing what's on view to keep the selection purposeful. But don't permanently purge pieces prematurely. Tuck special items you're not ready to part with into storage to rediscover for future display.

Like our relationships, accomplishments, and milestones, sentimental décor evolves as our lives progress. Allow your displays to elegantly reflect each passing era, what remains constant, and what falls away. Curate mindfully.

Selecting Your Signature Color Scheme

One of the most pivotal decisions when embracing dopamine décor is determining which vibrant color palette reflects your spirit and showcases your personality. While trendy "Color of the Year" paint hues come and go, your signature color scheme should remain true to you.

Start by revisiting meaningful colors tied to treasured memories and positive emotions. Which hues fill you with joy and come to mind when recalling beloved people, places, or times? Use these as jumping off points for selecting your core palette.

Beyond nostalgic colors, also factor in:

- Favorite Colors - Which hues have you been consistently drawn to since childhood? Stay true to longtime loves.

- Mood Enhancement - Seek out tones known to boost spirits like sunshine yellow, verdant green, and tranquil blue.

- PersonalMeaning - Choose colors representing causes or organizations important to you.

- Artwork Colors - Pull out unifying shades from cherished paintings or prints.

- Nature Inspiration - Mimic uplifting hues from stunning sunsets, landscapes, and blooms.

- Cultural Heritage - Incorporate colors celebrated within your ethnic background.

- Wardrobe Staples - Echo the palette of flattering clothing you gravitate toward.

Once you land on your core color scheme, display it abundantly throughout your home. Paint walls in your favorite tone, then layer in accent shades through textiles, accessories, and art. Upholding a coherent color story will create harmony and cohesion even when using eclectic pieces.

Here are additional tips for selecting and applying your color palette:

- Limit your palette to 3-5 core hues for cohesion.

- Showcase one dominant color, supported by complementary accent shades.

- Use color grouping and repetition to allow hues to build upon one another.

- Choose palettes with contrasting accent colors for visual dynamism.

- Incorporate patterns and textures in palette colors for depth.

- Mix sheens like matte, satin, and high-gloss in coordinated colors.

Establishing Color Cohesion

A common rookie error is selecting a motley crew of clashing colors that compete rather than complement. While an eclectic palette is encouraged, ensure some method to the color madness.

Start by choosing a leading color that figures most prominently. For example, if passionate red is your signature shade, use it abundantly on walls, furnishings, throws, and accents.

Now identify 2-3 accent colors to sprinkle throughout supporting your lead color. If red is primary, incorporate green and white as secondary hues. Repeat this colorful trio in varying saturations and patterns to tie spaces together cohesively.

Additional strategies for harmonious palettes include:

- Groupings in threes: triadic or tertiary color schemes featuring color families separated by equal distances on the color wheel.

- Analogous palettes: hues located right next to each other on the color wheel, such as blue, blue-violet, and violet.

- Coordinated warm or cool palettes: staying within a single color temperature family.

- Contrasting palettes: vivid accents against neutrals like teal and camel or fuchsia and grey.

- Just be sure to uphold balance. You want a spirited palette, not a jarring cacophony of mismatched colors competing for dominance.

Here are more cohesion tips:

- Repeat your signature colors in different gloss finishes: matte walls, glossy accent pillows.

- Incorporate patterns and prints in palette colors: floral sheets, striped curtains, buffalo check pillows.

- Unify rooms through color blocking: a green bedroom flows into a green and white kitchen.

- Use 60-30-10 formula: 60% dominant hue, 30% secondary, 10% accent shades.

Curating a personalized yet polished palette requires color coordination. But you needn't opt for cookie cutter matching to achieve cohesion. Thoughtfully repeating signature shades creates flow.

Color Placement Strategy

With a cohesive color palette selected, now determine strategic placement to maximize the mood-enhancing impact. Use accent walls, furniture, textiles and accessories to splash color abundantly.

Some suggestions include:

Living Spaces:

- Paint walls in warm hues like peach, yellow or green to cultivate cheer. Or opt for blues and purples to relax.

- Choose a vibrant sofa or accent chair as a bold splash of color.

- Add colorful pillows, throws, rugs and drapes to layer in accent shades.

- Select vibrant art, accessories and floral arrangements in coordinating colors.

Kitchens/Dining Rooms:

- Incorporate energizing red and orange accessories and appliances.

- Paint cabinets or the island in your signature shade.

- Showcase glassware, dishes and linens in themed colors.

- Use dining chairs or bar stools in a fun accent color.

Bedrooms:

- Paint walls in soothing blue or green tones to relax.

- Choose bedding, drapes and area rugs in coordinating accent colors.

- Add vibrant art and cheerful floral bouquets.

- Display meaningful photos and memorabilia in coordinating frames.

Bathrooms:

- Paint or wallpaper walls in sea glass hues like aqua, teal or blue.

- Display towels, bath mats, shower curtains and accessories in accent colors.

- Incorporate glass vessels, bottles and ceramics in coordinating hues.

Workspaces:

- Paint an energizing citrus hue like yellow, peach or grass green.

- Choose colorful desk accessories, organizational pieces, art.

- Showcase meaningful photos, art and memorabilia in coordinating frames.

- Get creative and intentional with color placement throughout your space. The psychology of color is powerful, so make the most of its elevating impact in areas where you want to feel calm, focused, energized or inspired. Use your palette expressively and unapologetically.

Chapter 3: Decorating with Color

Harnessing the Science of Color Psychology

While often overlooked, the deliberate use of color is one of the most powerful tools at your disposal for instantly shifting the overall mood and energy of a space. Extensive research confirms color directly impacts our emotions, behaviors, and physiological responses. So wielding color intentionally allows you to design feel-good environments that uplift and inspire.

Each hue possesses its own persuasive psychology and symbolism based on cultural associations and spiritual meanings accrued over centuries. While personal color preferences vary, general trends emerge:

- **Red** - This bold, passionate hue is inherently stimulating and high-energy. Red increases circulation and raises blood pressure, speeding up respiration and heart rate. It boosts excitement, appetite, and conversation, making it perfect for social spaces like dining rooms and lounges. Red provokes romance and intimacy as well, ideal for bedrooms. And it promotes productivity and focus, helpful in active workspaces.

- **Pink** - Universally associated with femininity, romance, and innocence, soft pinks have an innate sense of warmth, playfulness, and whimsy. These tender hues promote relaxation and diffuse feelings of aggression or anxiety. Light pinks create welcoming bedrooms, living rooms, and spas. Vibrant hot pinks add fun pops of color. Pink inspires nurturing vibes, ideal for children's spaces.

- **Orange** - This vibrant, cheerful hue combines the energy of red with the joy of yellow. Associated with enthusiasm and creativity, orange boosts mood, socialization, and communication. It sparks productive yet playful energy, perfect for shared workspaces. Orange adds warmth to any room. Use it to create an energetic, inspiring entryway. For kids' spaces, orange promotes learning and self-expression.

- **Yellow** - The quintessential color of sunshine, happiness, and optimism, yellow boosts serotonin and dopamine levels while activating memory and motivation. It aids concentration yet also provides relief from fatigue and anxiety. Use energetic yellow in workspaces to sharpen focus. Soft yellows create cheerful, welcoming kitchens and living rooms. Yellow inspires hope and confidence.

- **Green** - Universally associated with nature, renewal, stability, and tranquility, green possesses healing properties that reduce anxiety and promote balance. Sage greens cultivate peaceful bedrooms, while vivid greens energize exercise spaces. Green aids vision health, ideal for home offices. And it stimulates creativity, perfect for art studios. Surround yourself with green to create sanctuary.

- **Blue** - Cool, calming shades of blue lower heart rate and relax the mind, aiding concentration and inspiringreflection. Use blue in bedrooms to promote deep sleep and in offices to enhance productivity. Soft powder blues create serene, ethereal spa spaces. Navy blues lend spaces intimacy and subtle drama. Blue conjures images of soothing water.

- **Purple** - Traditionally a color of luxury, creativity, and mystery, purple provokes imagination and introspection. On the energetic side, vivid violets and fuchsia inject fun and whimsy, perfect for playrooms. Deeper eggplants and lilacs inspire contemplation and spiritual wisdom, ideal for meditation spaces. Allow purple to unlock your creativity.

Layering bright, optimistic hues establishes an uplifting backdrop while neutral walls allow accent colors to pop. When selecting your palette, consider how each hue impacts your mood and energy. Design your environment to nurture positive emotions.

Here are additional tips for effectively applying color:

- Saturate walls, textiles, and decor abundant in your favorite hues.

- Choose warmer tones like coral, peach, saffron for high-energy spaces.

- Incorporate cooler hues like sage, periwinkle, mint in relaxing spaces.

- Use darker shades to create intimate, cocooning spaces.

- Apply lighter tones in tight spaces to evoke spaciousness.

- Highlight architectural details by painting them in contrasting colors.

- Add pops of brightness with citrine, turquoise, and neon accents.

While many avoid strong color out of fear it will overwhelm, done right, it achieves the opposite - colorful rooms feel uplifting, playful, and alive. Don't shy away from boldness. Surround yourself with vibrant pigments that kindle joy.

Keep in mind that color perception depends on lighting. Use soft bulbs, illuminated paints, and natural light to make colors appear crisp yet inviting. And apply color thoughtfully in layers - don't overwhelm with competing hues in every finish and accessory. Allow each shade space to make an impact.

Above all, choose a color palette aligned with your personality and preferences, not fleeting trends. Seek out tones imbued with personal symbolism and meaning. Reestablish an emotional connection with color rooted in your childhood favorites and most treasured memories. Your home offers a chance to unapologetically embrace the hues that rouse your spirit.

Selecting Your Soul-Soothing Palette

One of the most pivotal steps in curating feel-good spaces is defining a cohesive color palette that reflects your spirit. When choosing your signature shades, look inward to identify hues that hold deep personal meaning and elicit positive emotions.

Ask yourself:

- Which colors spark joy and lift my mood?

- Which tones do I associate with beloved memories and places?

- Which hues have I been consistently drawn to since childhood?

- Which colors align with causes or organizations I support?

- Which shades match my complexion and flatter my skin tone?

Also extract color inspiration from:

- Your collection of cherished artwork and prints

- Stunning sunrises, sunsets, natural landscapes

- Heritage flags and textiles connected to your family backgrounds

- Your cultural traditions and celebrations

Once you've gathered inspiring colors, narrow down your signature palette to 3-5 complementary core hues. Choosing a focused color scheme creates harmony and cohesion even when decorating eclectically.

Here are ways to effectively apply your hand-picked palette:

- Use one dominant hue throughout, supported by accent shades

- Incorporate palette colors into wall paint, textiles, furniture, art

- Echo colors through pattern mixing and layered textures

- Choose a palette with contrasting accent colors for visual dynamism

- Mix sheens like matte, satin, metallic, high-gloss in coordinated hues

- Add warmth with wood tones and cream accents to balance bold colors

When implementing your color scheme, uphold balance and avoid overwhelming spaces with competing hues. Allow each shade room to make an impact through thoughtful grouping and repetition.

While trends come and go, your signature color palette should remain true to your spirit. Curate combinations that boost your mood and prompt fond recollections. Remember, the colors we surround ourselves with subconsciously influence our mindset and emotional state.

Here are additional tips for applying your personal palette:

- Use light, bright hues to make small spaces feel more open

- Incorporate darker, moodier tones in large rooms or to create intimacy

- Paint architectural details like moldings in contrasting colors for emphasis

- Add pops of brightness with citrine, chartreuse, fuchsia accents

- Incorporate metallic sheens like gold, rose gold, bronze for warmth

The colors you choose for your home should bring you delight when applied artfully to your walls, textiles, furnishings, and finishes. Decorating with purposeful palettes infuses your space with positive psychology and emotion. So embrace colors vibrantly and unapologetically - not those dictated by trends.

Selecting Colors that Spark Joy

When curating your custom color palette, start by identifying hues that spark positivity and joy within you. Tap into your memories and emotions to pinpoint special shades tied to treasured times, places and people from your past.

For example, buttercream yellow may elicit fond memories of the cheery kitchen in your grandma's beach cottage. Robin's egg blue evokes carefree childhood days spent by the lake each summer. Pumpkin spice orange reminds you of glorious autumn afternoons jumping in leaf piles with your siblings.

Make a list of all the nostalgic colors that come to mind when reliving your happiest memories. These sentimental shades already evoke heartwarming emotions within you, making them ideal candidates for your signature palette.

In addition to nostalgic hues, note colors you've felt consistently drawn to since childhood. Maybe you adored glittering pink growing up and still gravitate toward fuschia tones today. Or you were obsessed with rainbow brights as a kid. Stay true to lifelong color loves.

Spend time gathering swatches, paint strips, magazine clippings, and photographs showcasing your initial color contenders. Viewing these shades together will help guide you toward a cohesive palette. But first, gather possibilities unfiltered. Identifying sentimental, joy-sparking colors lays the foundation.

Curating Your Color Happy Place

In addition to nostalgic shades, look to your most cherished sanctuaries, both places dreamed of and destinations experienced, for rich color inspiration when designing your signature palette.

Make a list of all the places real or imagined that represent your version of color happy. These should be spaces you mentally retreat to when you need an infusion of lightness and joy.

For example, your color happy places might be:

- A vibrant coral reef, swathed in dazzling turquoise waters

- A cozy reading nook filled with books, sunshine pouring in the window

- A flower-filled meadow buzzing with butterflies on a summer's day

- An Italian villa with cheerful ocher walls and terra cotta roof tiles

- A white sand Caribbean beach with teal waves and azure skies

- A charming cottage kitchen painted peppy cherry red

- An alpine chalet retreat surrounded by evergreen trees after fresh snowfall

Now close your eyes and visualize each beloved color happy place in your mind's eye. Make notes on the colors that dominate each scene. These intrinsically uplifting shades will provide inspiration as you curate combinations guaranteed to boost your mood.

Aim to reflect the palette of places tied to positive emotions - tropical motifs in ocean blues and seafoam greens, florals in cherry pink, lime and violet, forested hues of deep emerald and earthy brown. Allow deeply meaningful colors to guide your selections.

Choosing an Uplifting Color Scheme

With an array of inspiring colors gathered from nostalgic memories and color happy places, you can now begin thoughtfully curating your signature palette.

Aim for 3-5 core hues that complement each other beautifully. For example sunny yellow as your dominant shade, coupled with sky blue and leafy green accent colors.

Keep the combinations uplifting and energizing by focusing on shades known to boost serotonin, creativity and mood like citrus yellows, vibrant greens, tranquil blues and vermillion reds. Avoid an overabundance of cool, moody tones.

Be sure to cross-reference paint swatches on walls throughout daylight hours. Colors appear different in morning light versus evening. View swatches in each room to ensure your palette feels cohesive throughout your home.

Most importantly, remain authentically you. Resist trendy "color of the year" hues unless they truly resonate. Your signature shades should ignite your spirit and prompt joyful memories, not impress design judges. Curate the palette that makes YOUR heart sing.

While some spaces demand conservative hues, your home offers a chance to finally embrace your most vibrant self through color. So give yourself full creative license. Remember, surrounding yourself with uplifting pigments lifts your mood.

Establishing Color Cohesion

Once you've identified your joy-sparking signature color scheme, maintain visual harmony by adhering to basic color theory principles:

- Use a dominant color abundantly supported by two accent hues

- Incorporate all palette colors into accompanying patterns and prints

- Echo colors in varying sheens: glossy green accents against flat matte green walls

- Repeat colors in proper proportions like the 60-30-10 rule

- Group colors in tertiary or triadic schemes with equidistant tones on the wheel

- Build analogous palettes using neighboring hues like teal, sage green, sky blue

- Contrast warm and cool palettes for vibrant pairings like peach and turquoise

The goal is a spirited yet soothing palette - not a jarring cacophony competing colors. Thoughtfully balance your signature shades through intentional repetition and coordinating accents.

Here are additional cohesion strategies:

- Incorporate black and white to sharpen bold colors without clashing

- Use wood tones like oak or walnut to warm up cool color palettes

- Add sophisticated depth by mixing matte and metallic finishes of the same hue

- Ground bright accents with neutral linens, furniture and area rugs as foundation

- Follow intuition when initially selecting colors. Then refine the combinations using harmonizing techniques for a polished, uplifting palette.

Injecting Brightness with Thoughtful Accents

While saturated wall colors establish an uplifting backdrop, sprinkling in vivid pops of accent hues keeps spaces feeling fresh, lively, and energized. Bold and unexpected splashes of color add visual dynamism, joyfully energizing rooms anchored in lighter neutrals.

Vibrant accents add layers of interest while creating unlikely color combinations that catch the eye and spark delight. Groupings of complementary brights provide an energetic counterpoint to otherwise calm spaces.

Here are ways to artfully incorporate pops of color as accents:

- Display brightly hued artwork, textiles, ceramics to inject color

- Add bright-colored dramatic lighting like crimson or sapphire pendant lights

- Incorporate neon and fluorescent accents in framing, vases, stationery

- Paint interior doors or architectural trim in a vivid contrasting color

- Use boldly colored furnishings like emerald green velvet sofas or citron chairs

- Layer in eye-catching throw pillows, blankets, and cushions on neutral beds/sofas

- Scatter bright rug accents like hot pink sheepskins or graphic orange mats

- Choose vivid kitchen appliances and décor in shades like cobalt, vermillion, and gold

- Showcase vibrant potted botanicals like fuchsia orchids or chartreuse succulents

- Hang faceted, colorful crystal prisms near windows to cast rainbow light

When applying pops of color:

- Focus on one accent color per room for cohesion

- Anchor brights with plenty of white and natural wood tones

- Use accents sparingly to prevent overwhelmingly spaces

- Add color in manageable doses through art, textiles, flowers

- Choose hues that complement your core color scheme

While neutrals and wood tones provide an organic, soothing foundation, vivid accents enliven rooms in subtly vibrant ways. Pops of color introduce thrilling contrast without overpowering. They provide necessary punctuation to counterbalance lighter backgrounds.

Most importantly, choose accent colors purely based on which hues elicit joy and positivity. Ignore trends and let color psychology guide your pairings. Combine tones known to lift your mood.

Squeeze every ounce of visual intrigue from your bright accents by backlighting colored glass vases and artwork or illuminating them with strategic spotlighting. This makes colors glow and appear richer. Surrounding yourself with electrifying pops boosts energy and mood while showcasing your bold spirit.

Chapter 4: Layering in Texture

Understanding the Power of Touch

While color and visual interest grab our attention initially, texture adds critical depth and dimension through the sense of touch. Dopamine décor leverages our human instinct to reach out and interact with pleasing textures. The addition of natural materials we crave stroking creates inviting warmth.

On a subconscious level, we are drawn to soothing, organic textures that evoke feelings of comfort, ease, and pleasure. Our minds associate tactile materials with relaxation and joy.

Consider why we flock to silk, cashmere, wood, leather, velvet, and wool:

- Soft, smooth textures relax and destress - Gentle stroking motions calm the nervous system. Caressing velvet, silk, or fleece soothes anxiety.

- Rough, nubby textures offer comfort - Coarse woven textures like bouclé fabric satisfy our craving for comforting physical touch.

- Natural textures feel innately pleasing - Materials derived from nature, like wood, cotton, and wool appeal to our senses.

- Familiar textures elicit nostalgia - Fabrics worn since childhood, like denim and linen prompt fond memories through touch.

- Novel, intriguing textures captivate us - Unusual tactile discoveries like sequins and fringe capture our curiosity.

In dopamine décor, choose pieces with pleasing physical properties you long to touch again and again. Seek out furnishings with inherent softness that entice interaction. Prioritize natural fibers, woven patterns, and cozy knits.

Here are additional ways to incorporate tantalizing textures:

- Layer plush blankets, cushions, and pillows abundantly

- Drape textural throws and sheepskins across sofas

- Incorporate nubby, dimensional upholstery fabrics like bouclé and tweed

- Display natural elements like driftwood, stones, shells

- Add softness with velvet pillows, berber rugs, chenille throws

- Incorporate wooden furniture, trays, tabletop accents

- Hang tactile wall tapestries with macramé and tassels

- Choose furniture and fabrics with handcrafted imperfections

- Gather baskets of woven raffia, seagrass, rattan

By tapping into textures you long to touch again and again, you create living spaces filled with finishing that bring you comfort and delight while appealing to your senses. Surfaces imbued with soothing tactile properties relax the body and mind.

Enveloping Your Space in Cozy Textiles

In addition to plush textiles, incorporating materials straight from nature infuses spaces with cozy, organic texture and warmth. Natural accents like wood, rattan, bamboo, jute, and ceramic add delightful depth while connecting to the outdoors.

Wood

- No material is more warm, inviting, and universally beloved than wood. Salvaged wood adds rustic patina. Smooth sanded wood provides sleek contrast. Oak, walnut, teak, and mahogany all have different grains to appreciate. Use wood for shelving, furniture, flooring, and accent walls. The sound, smell, and aesthetic of wood is unparalleled.

- The natural variations, knots, grain patterns and color changes of wood bring unmatched visual interest and depth into spaces. Wood instantly infuses interiors with inviting nature-made texture.

Rattan

- With its tactile woven texture, rattan makes one-of-a-kind furnishings and accents. It has a lightweight, airy quality perfect for living spaces. Incorporate handwoven rattan headboards, cabinetry, trunks, chairs, and wall screens. The organic variations in rattan add natural beauty.

- From pillows and ottomans to mirror frames and bowls, rattan's intricate woven patterns make every piece unique. The pleasingly bumpy texture adds cozy tactile contrast against smooth walls and tabletops.

Jute

- As a fiber, jute possesses an earthy, burlap-like texture that brings cozy rusticity to any surface, from woven rugs and wall hangings to lampshade backing. Jute appeals to minimalists and maximalists alike with its neutral tones and nubby texture.

- Durable and naturally insulating, jute offers an affordable way to bring dimensional fiber texture into a space. Use jute baskets and rugs to provide depth without overwhelming visually.

Bamboo

- Bamboo can be pressed into pliable sheets for curvy furniture or woven into airy screens and mats. Bamboo communicates tranquility and flexibility through its tactile properties. Use bamboo furnishings and decor to soften hard edges.

- With its delicate natural grain variations, blonde bamboo brings a soothing warmth reminiscent of wood into spaces while contrasting sleekly against it. Bamboo conveys an element of peaceful Zen through its flexibility.

Ceramic

- From humble mugs to handbuilt vases, the cool, smooth, weighty texture of ceramic appeals to human senses. Ceramics bridge indoor and outdoor spaces. Work carved wooden bowls and ceramic tableware into kitchen and dining room displays.

- The pleasingly imperfect natural glazes and handmade variations of ceramic pieces bring artisanal soul into modern, maximalist and minimalist spaces alike. Ceramic's density provides comforting stability.

Concrete

- While hard and industrial, concrete takes on a soothing, grounding presence when polished into tile, decorative bowls, and tabletops. Concrete adds comforting mass and permanence. Use it indoors and out for an organic yet refined look.

- With their weighty stillness, concrete elements provide an earthy material contrast against light woods, airy rattans, and luscious textiles. The neutral tone plays well with any color scheme.

Stone

- Marble, travertine, granite, and other natural stones make stunning countertops, floors, walls, and decor. The visual depth, permanence, and veining found in natural stone is unparalleled. Let stone bring your spaces back to ancient roots.

● Beyond their enduring beauty, the density and coolness of natural stones grounds spaces with mineral calm. Each stone possesses mesmerizing depth that draws the eye in like an ocean tide pool. Their permanence provides stability.

When sourcing natural materials, seek out repurposed and reclaimed wood, as well as ethically harvested rattan, bamboo, and jute. Make every effort to preserve natural resources. Mixing natural textures together creates depth and dimension - pair stone tabletops with woven dining chairs, rattan carpets atop wooden flooring, ceramic planters on live edge tables. The blend of natural materials soothes the soul.

Here are more ways to infuse indoor rooms with organic accents:

● Hang woven palm leaf wall decor and bamboo window screens

● Display geode slices, agate coasters, and stone bookends

● Choose naturally dyed, undyed linen and cotton textiles

● Accent with handthrown pots and ceramic garden stools

● Illuminate spaces with room dividers, lanterns, and lamps of woven rattan or wood

● Craft wooden gallery walls to showcase art and beloved objects

● Layer cowhide rugs over jute carpeting for delightfully contrasting textures

● Add handcarved wooden figurines and decorative bowls

● Incorporate natural baskets woven from rattan, willow, straw

● Display collections of interesting stones, crystals and shells

● Use handmade clay or concrete vessels as vases and catchalls

● Accent with blocks of raw marble, travertine or wood cut into abstract sculptures

By thoughtfully blending natural materials you source sustainably, you satisfy the inherent human craving for exposure to unrefined, tactile elements from the natural world. Their textural properties relax the mind, body, and spirit.

The Warmth of Wood in Interior Spaces

Of all organic materials, wood reigns supreme in its universality beloved for its unmatched warmth and organic beauty. Here are some recommended uses for wood throughout interior spaces:

Living Spaces:

- Salvaged wood coffee tables with notes of rustic patina
- Smooth sanded wooden console tables to contrast textures
- Reclaimed wood entertainment unit housing TVs and devices
- Wood framed seating and furnishings for an inviting look
- Walnut wood accent wall with embedded shelving

Dining Rooms:

- Gorgeous live-edge wooden dining tables
- Textural wood plank ceilings overhead
- A set of wooden dining chairs with sculpted details
- Wood shelving built-in to display cherished dishware

Kitchens:

- Wood laminate cabinetry and drawers
- Chopping blocks and butcher block work surfaces
- Rustic wooden open shelving for loose kitchen items
- Suspended wooden pot racks free up counterspace

Bedrooms:

- Wood platform beds with built-in side tables
- Slatted wood headboards backing pillows

- Wooden bedside table, dresser and console surfaces

- Wood mounted bed canopy hung from the ceiling

Bathrooms:

- Gorgeous wood vanities topped with stone sinks

- Textural teak wood mats on the floor

- Wall-mounted reclaimed wood floating shelves

The natural variations, knots, grain patterns and color changes of wood bring unmatched visual interest and depth into spaces. Wood instantly infuses interiors with inviting nature-made texture.

Incorporating Rattan & Wicker Pieces

Beyond standard wooden furniture, incorporating woven rattan and wicker furnishings provides delightful organic texture. Rattan and wicker can be used to create:

- Headboards cushioned with pillows

- Nightstands and dressers with storage

- Beautiful handwoven bench seating with removable cushions

- Light and airy shelving units to hold belongings

- Lanterns, lamps and window screens filtering light

- Refined framed mirrors and artwork

- Woven ottomans and side tables

- Planters, vases, bowls and catchalls

- Ornate room dividers providing privacy

From pillows and ottomans to mirror frames and bowls, rattan's intricate woven patterns make every piece unique. The pleasingly bumpy texture adds cozy tactile contrast against smooth walls and tabletops.

For bamboo, possible uses include:

- Chair and table legs adding dimension

- Shelving units with adjustable heights

- Slatted window coverings for diffused light

- Woven mat flooring adding depth and texture

- Removable wall dividers to transform spaces

- Foldable privacy screens around bathtubs

With their delicate natural grain variations, blonde bamboo and rattan bring a soothing warmth reminiscent of wood into spaces while contrasting sleekly against it. These woven fibers convey an element of peaceful Zen through their flexibility.

Incorporating Ceramic & Terracotta

Beyond texture underfoot, ceramics add delightful smoothness, weight, and earthy glazed warmth to every surface they grace. Possible applications include:

- Vases and pots for fresh cut stems

- Handcrafted mugs and dishes for dining

- Catchall trays clustering small accessories

- Bowls holding everyday objects like keys

- Bookends and paperweights holding pages in place

- Surface touches like ceramic egg and figurine décor

- Garden stools that function as side tables

- Textural ceramic wall tiles for kitchen backsplashes

The pleasingly imperfect natural glazes and handmade variations of ceramic pieces bring artisanal soul into modern, maximalist and minimalist spaces alike. Ceramic's density provides comforting stability.

For terracotta and clay, potential uses include:

- Figurines and sculptural objects with artistic flair

- Textural tiles laid into kitchen, fireplace and bathroom surfaces

- Amphorae, planters and pots for housing plants

- Platters, cups, vases and kitchen canisters

Terracotta surfaces satisfyingly smooth to the touch while natural clay adds more organic, hand-thrown character and charm. The comforting orange-red earthiness feels pleasantly grounding.

Working Concrete and Stone Indoors

For smooth coolness paired with rugged permanence, concrete and natural stone add delightful contradiction and weighty texture. Possible applications include:

Concrete:

- Polished concrete floors with radiant heating

- Cast concrete features like fireplaces and bathtubs

- Concrete kitchen, bar and vanity countertops

- Poured concrete furnishings like tables, shelves and benches

- Decorative concrete bowls, vases, candle holders and trays

- Pressed concrete tile for backsplash accent walls and fireplaces

- Stone:

-

- Honed natural stone bathtubs, sinks, shower surrounds

- Gorgeous stained concrete floors with radiant heating

- Organic edged stone coffee and side tables

- Elegant marble, limestone and travertine fireplace surrounds

- Natural stone and marble kitchen surfaces and backsplashes

- Geodes and stone decor objects like bookends and sculptures

With their weighty stillness, concrete and stone elements provide an earthy material contrast against light woods, airy rattans, and luscious textiles. The neutral tone plays well with any color scheme.

Thoughtfully blending natural materials you source sustainably satisfies the inherent human craving for exposure to unrefined, tactile elements from the natural world. Their textural properties relax the mind, body, and spirit.

Bringing the Outdoors In with Natural Elements

Enveloping Your Space in Cozy Textiles

When designing for optimal texture and comfort underfoot and atop furnishings, fabrics reign supreme. Plush rugs, cushions, pillows, throws, and upholstery invite snuggling while introducing tantalizing visual and tactile diversity.

Dopamine décor capitalizes on our affection for touchable textiles by emphasizing abundantly layered natural fibers and sumptuous knits. Time-honored materials like cotton, wool, linen, and silk add organic coziness.

Cozy Textiles to Incorporate

Here are cozy fabrics and textiles to thoughtfully incorporate:

- Knit Throws - Chunky, handcrafted wool, alpaca, and cotton throws provide snug softness ideal for bed backs, sofas, and chairs. Opt for chunky knits with brushed interiors for optimal coziness. The weight of these throws makes them perfect for curling up with a book on a crisp evening or providing additional warmth on a chilly night.

- Woven Wool Rugs - Naturally insulating wool rugs add comforting cushioning and visual texture when underfoot. Wool's sound-absorbing properties also cut down on echos. The durability and stain-resistance of wool makes it suitable for high-traffic areas while its natural moisture-wicking properties help carpets wear well overtime.

- Velvet Pillows - With indulgent softness begging to be touched, velvet instantly elevates sofas and beds. Look for cotton-backed velvet that won't slip around. The luxurious texture gives rooms a glamorous feel and is comforting to rest against while reading or watching TV in bed.

- Cashmere Blankets - Known for unparalleled lightness and warmth, cashmere crafts heirloom-quality blankets. Seek out Mongolian cashmere for durability. Few materials can rival the buttery softness of cashmere against skin. Cashmere offers exceptional warmth without weight, making these opulent blankets perfect for elevating any sofa or bed.

- Mohair Throws - Made of angora goat hair, mohair possesses a fluffy, fuzzy texture perfect for cozying up in. Mohair brilliantly diffuses light, creating cozy ambiance. Delicately draping mohair throws over furniture addsinstant textural interest while also making the perfect portable wrap to keep nearby when the temperature drops.

- Chenille Pillows - With its signature tufted pile, chenille has an irresistibly soft, dimensional texture. Chenille resists fading, pilling, and crushing. The luxuriously soft and subtly iridescent sheen of chenille pillows adds plushness against sofa backs and headboards. Chenille is soft enough for comfort yet dense enough to provide ample support.

- Alpaca Throws - Hypoallergenic and thermal regulating, alpaca throws provide extraordinary softness. Alpaca rivals cashmere for softness at a more affordable price point. Amazingly lightweight yet cozy, alpaca fiber makes the ultimate cold weather companion draped over shoulders or laps. The softness also makes alpaca ideal for cradling babies.

- Llama Wool Rugs - Llama wool makes plush yet durable rugs that insulate and delight. Llama wool contains no lanolin so it won't aggravate allergies. Llama fiber equals wool in softness and warmth but resists pilling. The natural insulation helps retain heat in rooms. Llama wool rugs become softer and more lustrous with age.

- Silk Pillowcases - Unquestionably luxurious and gentle against skin and hair, silk makes indulgent bedding. Mulberry silk offers the longest-lasting quality. The ultra-smooth surface of silk prevents sleep creases and tangles by allowing hair to glide across pillows. Silk's moisture-wicking properties help keep skin hydrated overnight.

When sourcing fabrics, seek out natural fibres like wool, cotton, linen, and silk which feel comforting against skin. Prioritize durability and craftsmanship to build keepsakes that last generations. Shop for textiles that can be frequently laundered to maintain freshness and vibrancy.

Using fabrics thoughtfully allows you to tailor rooms to feel as plush and welcoming as your favorite sweater. Keep the following coziness goals in mind when selecting and arranging textiles:

- Warmth - This encompasses both tangible temperature regulation through insulation and the abstract feeling of emotional warmth through soft, familiar textures.

- Comfort - Fabrics should invite relaxing into, napping upon, and snuggling within. Soft, lightweight, breathable fibers feel best against skin.

- Safety - We instinctively seek spaces that envelop us in soothing softness away from the harshness of the world. Textiles provide this literal and symbolic protective barrier.

- Joy - Certain fabrics like cushy chenille, fuzzy mohair, supple velvet or linens evoke childhood contentedness. Textures elicit nostalgia.

- Belonging - When we wrap ourselves in blankets passed down generations or sit atop heirloom rugs, textiles ground us in family traditions spanning time and space.

- Infusing rooms with meaningful, responsibly sourced fabrics allows you to surround yourself with coziness, comfort, joy and familial belonging.

Incorporating Textural Layers

Now let's explore thoughtful ways to welcome sumptuous fibers into your interiors:

- Upholstery - Sofas and chairs deserve special attention as centerpieces. Chenille, bouclé, velvet and leather make ideal soft yet durable choices. Opt for removable slipcovers to refresh.

- Rugs - Layer flatweave, shag and sheepskin varieties for multi-textural flooring. Alternate wall-to-wall with area rugs underfoot.

- Pillows - Accent sofas and beds with pillows in an array of plush fabrics like velvet, mohair and linen. Mix sizes and textures.

- Throws - Drape custom-knit cotton, alpaca and wool throws over chair and sofa backs. Fold at the foot of beds.

- Blankets - Choose special blankets like handwoven quilts or cashmere heirlooms to display proudly at the end of beds to layer color and texture.

- Window Treatments - Hang tactile drapes and curtains in natural linen, cotton, and velvet to soften windows and filter light gracefully.

- Beds - Dress mattresses in soothing eileen fisher linen sheets topped with cozy textural blankets and pillows aplenty.

● Wall Accents - Incorporate handwoven tapestries, macrame hangings and textural whitewashed wood panels for depth.

● Seating Accents - Toss sheepskin throws over leather chairs or position embroidered floor poufs around spaces for flexible comfort.

● Dining - Set tables with cloth napkins, woven placemats and your best vintage tablecloths to envelop meals in textile warmth.

Here are additional ways to infuse rooms with fabric texture:

● Choose upholstery in tactile natural fabrics like bouclé, tweed, or corduroy

● Layer rug textures and fabrics - flatweave under shag under sheepskin

● Incorporate fabric wall panels, headboards, macramé wall hangings

● Display beautifully bound books and leather goods

● Showcase heirloom table linens, tapestries, and quilts

● Add dimensionality with fabric draping, gathering, and ruching

● Mix sheens like matte cotton, lustrous velvet, shiny satin

● Accent with embroidered and embellished fabric objects like toss pillows and poufs

● Soften hard edges and surfaces with textural throws and upholstered ottomans

● Contrast airy sheers with cozy opaque window treatments

● Incorporate texturally intriguing basketry, ropes, and wood weavings

Curating a thoughtful blend of new and vintage textiles creates depth and visual interest while providing endless comfort. Limit synthetics which lack natural breathability and temperature control. The sensations of wrapping ourselves in comforting textiles satisfies our perpetual craving for coziness.

Choosing Durable Upholstery Fabrics

As the anchor pieces and workhorses of most spaces, upholstered furnishings deserve special durability consideration:

- Opt for tightly woven, high-rub count cottons that resist pilling and stand up well to everyday use.

- Wool blends add comforting texture and inherent stain resistance. Seek out tightly twisted, dense yarns.

- Heavyweight linens like Belgian linen offer refined luxury and gain character over time. The tighter the weave, the more durable.

- Durable synthetics like nubby polyester herringbone give the tactile appearance of wool or linen at more accessible price points.

- For family-friendly spaces, performance velvets and chenilles withstand constant use. Spot clean regularly.

- Leather offers endless durability and softens beautifully overtime. Opt for full-grain over woven splits which can crack. Top-grain is mid-range.

- Microfibers like microsuede provide plush softness perfect for cushions. Avoid delicate microfibers on seats or backs.

- Prioritize timeless over trendy. A chesterfield sofa in rich leather or a classically chic linen Lawson sofa will gracefully stand the test of time and wear. Seek out better-quality frames with corner-block joinery and avoid lower cost particleboard.

While ultra contemporary shapes feel exciting initially, classic silhouettes remain reliably stylish for years on end. Choose thoughtfully constructed furnishings in durable fabrics that only gain more character with use. You invest in pieces to last a lifetime.

Handcrafting Custom Throws

For truly special custom throws, consider commissioning textile artist studios where artisans skillfully handcraft knits. While pricier, these become instant heirlooms. Or opt to thrift vintage finds like embroidered Turkish flatweaves rich with heritage.

When custom knitting, select from fibers like organic wool, baby alpaca, cashmere, or mohair then decide on stitches. Looser open knits work in milder climates while tighter stitches provide warmth. You may incorporate special fibers like qiviut, angora, or pashmina for added luxury.

Next, focus on shape, proportion, length, and finishing. Do you prefer a luxe oversized toss silhouette or more tailored throws? Contrasting blanket stripes and borders add interest. Personalize with meaningfully selected colors and incorporate any special embellishments like your family initials or special dates.

The beauty of bespoke blankets is their ability to personalize through fibers, textures, colors and details you cherry pick. Custom throws become cherished keepsakes anticipated for generations. Worthy investments, they promise to elevate any space immediately with their skillful handmade charm.

Rug Layering for Multi-Textural Flooring

An easy way to instantly infuse more tactile coziness underfoot is through multi-textural rug layering. Combining varying rugs creates a more plush, visually intriguing surface. Benefits include:

- Added insulation - Layering rugs traps air, making spaces feel toastier

- Sound absorption - Softer piled rugs help absorb noise and echos

- Custom combinations - Curate special color and texture mixes like jute and wool

- Tie larger and smaller rugs together - Layering prevents shifting

- Protects pricier rugs underneath - Top rugs shield investment pieces

- Elevates thin or inexpensive rugs - More affordable rugs gain richness layered

Aim for contrasting textures and weaves when stacking rugs for the biggest visual impact. For example:

- Flatweave jute or dhurrie rugs topped with fluffy sheepskins

- Natural sisal rugs under wool kilims or shag rugs

- Simple hemp and rag weaves topped with ornate vintage carpets

Get creative combining varying fibers, weaves, and pile lengths to craft custom flooring that looks and feels abundantly lush. Just be sure to anchor top rugs properly to avoid slippage between layers.

Thoughtfully Curating Fabric Collections

To prevent your space from skewing cluttered, thoughtfully edit and arrange your fabric collection:

Color Pair Down

- Limit colorways to a cohesive palette so textiles feel cohesively collected, not haphazard. For example, softly color coordinate your throw pillows and blankets.

Style in Vignettes

- Cluster pillows, blankets and other textiles in artful vignettes around furnishings. Group items with intention, not just scattered randomly.

Control Clutter

- Store excess off-season textiles like coats or quilts away to prevent overwhelming spaces. Rotate pieces seasonally.

Vintage Variety

- Blend old and new textures like displaying heirloom quilts on minimalist beds or topping sleek chairs with handwoven pillows.

Folded Just So

- Neatly fold and display blankets at the foot of sofas or beds. Experiment with origami-like folds. Blankets kept askew appear messier.

Elevate Arrangements

- Use baskets, storage ottomans and wall hooks to neatly corral items when not in use. Conceal clutter.

While amassing abundant cozy textiles brings comfort, orderly displays keep the focus on selected standouts. Curate your collection thoughtfully to highlight special pieces in artful arrangements and vignettes.

The sensory experience of enveloping ourselves in beloved fabrics satisfies our inherent craving for coziness and contentment. Thoughtfully incorporating touches of cuddly textural bliss energizes interior spaces with Zhang vitality. Surround yourself in treasured fibers and natural textures.

Chapter 5: Displaying Cherished Items

Curating your memorabilia and keepsakes

More than any décor trend, the heart of dopamine design lies in proudly displaying nostalgic memorabilia imbued with sentimental significance. Curating these cherished keepsakes injects spaces with personality and soul.

Seek out mementos tied to beloved memories and relationships. Photographs, souvenirs, family heirlooms, and childhood treasures each tell part of your unique story. Artfully arrange touches from the past to inspire recollection of adventures, celebrations, and those you hold dear.

Photographs

Frame collections of sentimental moments capturing loved ones, monumental events, and favorite faraway places. Display any wedding portraits, candid family shots, senior photos, or professional sessions commemorating key milestones.

Include a thoughtful range of sizes, black and white alongside color. Arrange framed prints together in polished gallery walls or casually clustered groupings. Tuck some favorite snapshots into books as bookmarks. And choose frame styles that complement your broader décor approach.

When curating special photographs, consider framing:

- Portraits of grandparents, parents, siblings, children, and grandchildren that honor lineage

- Cherished photos with best friends that convey meaningful relationships

- Picturesque scenes from adventures near and far that ignite wanderlust

- Images capturing your home through the years to appreciate its evolution

- Candid moments revealing personality and spontaneity frozen in time

- Photography allows us to vividly relive treasured memories and celebrate connections that matter most. Take care to purposefully showcase meaningful captured instants.

Childhood Art

Preserve favorite drawings, paintings, pottery, sculptures, and school art projects from your youth or your children's developmental years. Neatly frame or display these creative artifacts on the refrigerator to appreciate the creativity, self-expression, and innocence of childhood.

Your inner child will smile knowing their early artistic contributions still have an appreciated place in your heart and home. Cherish the whimsy and unrestrained imagination of budding young artists.

Possible ways to showcase child art include:

- Framing exceptional pieces to display like gallery art

- Creating a child art gallery wall showcasing a collection of favorites

- Covering a bulletin board or corkboard in an array of creative works

- Scanning special masterpieces to reprint onto decorative pillows, mugs or stationery

- Letting children curate rotating "art museum" exhibits

- By honoring childhood creativity, you encourage artistic ingenuity and self-assurance. Displaying early artwork nurtures confidence and allows children to see their efforts recognized.

Awards & Trophies

Exhibit hard-earned academic honors, athletic victories, and career accomplishments via the trophies, medals, ribbons, plaques and regalia you've accumulated. For students, carefully display medals, academic regalia like diplomas, and science fair awards. For athletes, showcase trophies and framed team jerseys.

These recognitions validate past struggles and efforts while motivating future achievements. They commemorate the diligence, discipline and determination you've exemplified pursuing your ambitions.

Possible display ideas include:

- Wall shelves lined with trophies from various pursuits

- Floating wall ledges exhibiting academic regalia

- Shadowboxes containing medals, pins and ribbons grouped by pursuit

- Display cases spotlighting nostalgic awards and milestones

- Framed jerseys, oars, or equipment from past sports seasons

- Bulletin boards upon which badges and patches can be pinned

- By giving achievements prominence, you inspire yourself and others to continue excelling and reaching worthy goals that make a difference.

Musical Instruments

Display musical instruments from childhood lessons or bands played in during your youth. Mount special violins, guitars, trumpets, clarinets or drum sets on the wall as artistic focal points. Drape vintage band uniforms nearby.

Showcasing your musical background displays well-rounded interests and conveys your lifelong creative spirit. Visitors immediately perceive you as musically inclined and multi-talented.

Ways to artfully incorporate instruments include:

- Hanging guitar or ukulele wall mounts with instruments ready to play

- Using special drum sets or cellos as sculptural accents in offices or living rooms

- Building a customized paneled wall with instruments mounted within each section

- Creating a "band practice corner" with mic stands, amps, and instruments on display

- Framing vintage band posters and glamour shots alongside instruments

- Let your talents shine. The instruments you've mastered reflect commitment, creativity, and passion.

Collections

Display any sets of objects you've gathered through the years that hold nostalgic significance or document favorite pursuits. These could include seashells, classic cars, miniature buildings, ticket stubs, rare postage stamps, vintage clothing, or handcrafted trinkets passed down through generations.

Collections reflect your personal interests, quirky curiosities and what captures your fancy. Group like items together in framed collages, shelves, or glass cabinets for visitors to admire and explore. Add framed captions or labels explaining the significance behind certain pieces.

Possible collection display ideas include:

- Shadowboxes containing all found sea glass or smoothed stones from beach vacations past

- Curio cabinets showcasing your owl figurine collection

- Baseball card collections in specialty binders exhibited on edge facing outward

- Vintage postcards or pulp novel covers neatly framed in gridded arrangements

- Miniature model cars, trains, or houses encased in glass shelves

- Display cases spotlighting rare stamps, trading cards, or comic books

- Let your treasures reveal the tales of who you are and what thrills you. There's artistry in assembling aesthetically pleasing collections.

Travel Souvenirs

Demonstrate your lifelong love of adventure and cultures worldwide through the travel souvenirs, photos, maps, tickets, and curiosities you've gathered. Arrange related objects from certain voyages together artfully in frames, shadowboxes or shelves.

For example, display Eiffel Tower miniatures, French market flowers, Parisian postcards and franc notes collected on a memorable couples' getaway to France on a dedicated shelf. Or showcase stone carvings, bangles and textiles from a soul-stirring solo backpacking trip through India in a shadowbox.

Grouped displays allow you to recount memorable experiences from past expeditions while inspiring dreams of future excursions and wonder at the kaleidoscope of global cultures.

Possible displays include:

- A case of shells, starfish, pearls, and coral from beach vacations

- Vintage maps, compasses, and train tickets from cross-country adventures

- Framed montages of pressed flowers and leaves from hikes in the Alps

- A juried case of stones, gems and geodes gathered from exotic locales

- Handmade masks, textiles and crafts collected from indigenous artisans

- Let your displays transport guests across continents as they admire artifacts and listen to travel tales.

Antique Furnishings

Incorporate furniture, lighting, or decorative pieces passed down through your family that hold lineage meaning. Refinish and subtly modernize heirloom furnishings like tables or secretaries by reupholstering or repainting while still preserving their legacy.

Antique furnishings recount your ancestry and connection to past eras. While adding vintage flair, they also feel imbued with the spirits of those that came before you. Use them lovingly to add a touch of heritage charm.

Possible heirloom uses include:

- Wooden display hutches or curio cabinets exhibiting heirloom dishware

- Vintage desk chairs that offer a comforting sense of history while you work

- A treasured steamer trunk at the foot of a bed or styled as a coffee table with cushions on top

- Refinished mid-century carts or tables serving as quirky side tables

- Gallery walls decorated with ornate antique frames around meaningful family photos

- Let special pieces tell the story of your roots proudly on display. The patina of age only adds to their beloved charm.

Prized Books

Exhibit rare first editions, childhood favorites, Series of Unfortunate Events, Harry Potter books, signed copies by prominent authors or other prized volumes. Display them prominently on shelves or stacked invitingly on coffee tables. Let your library speak to your literary loves, ethics and interests.

Possible book display ideas include:

- Built-in bookshelves packed with volumes sorted by category, author, or color

- Floating ledges reaching up to the ceiling to accommodate overflowing collections

- Backless glass-faced bookcases keeping cherished titles visible

- Wheeled library carts holding books paired with reading nook armchairs

- A stack of beloved books and reading glasses left casually upon a side table

- Frames showcasing antique book covers, dust jackets or fanning page edges

- Surround yourself with knowledge, imaginative worlds, and cherished narratives. There's comfort in seeing the stories we love displayed artfully as décor.

Thoughtful Memorabilia Arrangement

When arranging your curated memorabilia displays, aim for creative, cohesive displays - not simply scattered clutter. Take measures to thoughtfully edit and preserve pieces:

- Only showcase items holding profound personal meaning or significance.

- Visually unify framed photos/art by repeating frame finishes, sizes or coordinating on color palettes.

- Contain and elevate items through shadowboxes, shelves, and display cases that protect from dust and damage.

- Group memorabilia together in neat thematic vignettes - for example, beach souvenirs together in one case.

- Add labels noting eras, relationships, and occasions commemorated to provide context.

- Balance precious artifacts from the past with items representing the present to reflect the continuum of life.

Displaying cherished relics allows you to relive treasured memories while expressing your multi-layered identity and story. Take care to arrange life mementos as artfully as you would any interior décor -with heart and intention.

Crafting Uplifting Photo Displays

One of the most powerful ways to infuse spaces with sentimentality is through abundantly displaying cherished photos of loved ones, alma maters, breathtaking vistas, and monumental milestones.

Dopamine décor encourages dedicating wall space to artistically arranged collections of meaningful images that prompt happy reminiscence.

Some tips:

- Photograph Frames - Choose frames in a cohesive style like silver metal, natural wood, or black matting. Metal frames add polish while wood communicates warmth. Mix frame shapes and sizes for dynamic arrangements.

- Candid Photos - Prioritize candid shots radiating authentic joy over posed portraits for intimate glimpses into relationships. Feature generations together - old photos alongside newborns.

- Creative Arrangements - Cluster frames asymmetrically rather than grid-like. Overlap frames for dimension. Hang them salon-style clustered near one another for impact.

- Thematic Grouping - Curate mini collections around beloved themes like family holidays, beach vacations, graduations, new homes, weddings, babies, and pets.

- Black & White Photography - Incorporate both black-and-white and color photography for visual interest. Vintage black and white portraits capture timeless nostalgia.

- Enlarge Special Photos - Spotlight extra special images as large statement pieces like 16x20" enlargements. This allows their emotional impact to shine.

- Photo Books - Intersperse framed photos with displayed photobooks and albums for interactive storytelling. Leave them out to flip through.

- Everyday Moments - Don't limit yourself to monumental events - capture candid everyday moments to remember simple joys: blowing bubbles, festive meals, playground time.

- Wall Design - Use framed photos to create installation art in unique shapes like a tree, geometric collage, or heart. Arrange them to mimic wall molding.

Settings that Inspired You - Feature scenic images of places that hold special significance: honeymoon beaches, childhood homes, college campuses, sanctuaries.

Beyond cherished photographs, personalized art prints and paintings bring positivity:

- Custom Signs - Display custom street signs featuring family last names, hometowns, established dates, motivational quotes.

- House Portraits - Commission artists to recreate portraits of homes past and present, ideal above a fireplace.

- Hand-Drawn Maps - Frame artistic renderings mapping important sites and travels like weddings, hometowns, alma maters.

- Watercolor Florals - Frame vivid painting of favorite flowers and botanicals. Vibrant blossoms represent growth.

- Uplifting Quotes - Add artwork and canvases spotlighting motivational quotes that lift your outlook and beliefs.

- Nostalgic Prints - Seek old-fashioned prints featuring beloved icons like vintage cars and historic landmarks.

- Song Lyrics - Frame meaningful stanzas from songs holding personal significance as artistic reminders.

By surrounding yourself with imagery tied to beloved times, places, accomplishments, and people, you infuse your space with nostalgic positivity. Display photos artfully to spotlight what matters most. Choose frames and arrangements amplifying the mood you desire - playful, peaceful, exuberant, cozy.

Most importantly, refresh your displays seasonally. Rotate in new moments captured across the years. Allow collections to evolve as life's adventures continue unfolding. Let your walls visually recount stories while inspiring the days yet to come.

Proudly Displaying Cherished Collections

Dopamine décor encourages proudly exhibiting personally curated collections that reflect your passions, interests, values and memories.

Displayed thoughtfully, assembled objects tell rich stories while revealing what captivates you.

When showcasing collections:

- Edit mindfully - Evaluate entire collections but selectively display most meaningful pieces. Avoid clutter.

- Organize logically - Group collection items together by type, date, color, size or theme.

- Elevate favorites - Spotlight particularly special pieces on their own pedestals or in framed cases.

- Label discreetly - Use small tags or plaques to identify pieces and their origin stories.

- Rotate seasonal - Refresh collection displays periodically to appreciate forgotten pieces.

- Illuminate dramatically - Use lighting to spotlight collectibles and amplify their details.

- Enhance interactivity - Allow visitors to gently handle collectibles to forge connections.

Types of collections you can proudly display:

- Memorabilia - Showcase ticket stubs, programs, pins, and other souvenirs from cherished events and travels.

- Coins & Stamps - Exhibit visually arresting coin and stamp collections in specialty albums and under glass frames.

- Figurines - Display collections of cherished figurines and statuettes, from Hummels to Precious Moments.

- Music Loves - Frame concert posters, vintage records, and signed albums from favorite bands.

- Sports Treasures - Display signed balls, jerseys, and equipment from favorite sports teams and athletes.

- Nature Finds - Create artistic arrangements of shells, stones, sand dollars, feathers, and driftwood discovered on adventures.

- Movie Memorabilia - Showcase ticket stubs, posters, autographed scripts and merch from beloved films.

- Historical Relics - Preserve interesting documents like newspapers announcing major events and old maps.

- Toys & Games - Proudly display favorite childhood games, trading cards, and iconic toys like LEGO sets.

- Books - Organize book collections by genre, subject, or color. Feature autographed editions and classics.

By proudly showcasing objects reflecting your interests, skills, values and origins, you surround yourself with daily inspiration while providing guests glimpses into your heart and spirit.

Collections represent accomplishments amassed gradually through determination. They communicate wisdom acquired, destinations reached, mementos gathered. Each piece tells a story. Each set formed reveals concentrated effort.

To prevent collections from appearing cluttered:

1. Curate designated display spaces like shadowboxes, cabinets, shelves
2. Limit collections to specific areas rather than scattering pieces throughout
3. Choose cohesive display vessels like baskets, frames, vessels in one color family
4. Arrange collections in orderly groupings - symmetrical or rainbow-ordered
5. Provide sufficient negative space around and between displayed objects
6. Adjust lighting to amplify collection details

With thoughtful presentation, collections become artistic installations expressing your essence. The act of assembling treasured sets helps satisfy our intrinsic need for gathering, organizing, and revisiting objects that sparked joy.

Surprisingly, displaying collections prominently can strengthen focus and productivity. Visually reviewing cherished collections reminds you of accomplishments attained through determination. This motivates ongoing pursuit of purpose.

Let your collections speak on your behalf, telling the story of who you are, where you've been and what you love most. Their presentation style reflects your personality while conversing on your behalf when you have guests.

Chapter 6: Pulling It All Together

Tying spaces together with color palettes

When embracing an eclectic blend of cherished memorabilia, global antiques, and vivid pops of color, upholding harmony can be challenging. The final step in curating a joyful home is pulling disparate spaces together visually using cohesive color palettes.

Implementing a consistent color scheme provides the common thread stitching rooms into a unified story even when décor varies wildly.

Here are tips for creating flow:

- Choose 3-5 core hues - Limit your signature palette to a few complementary colors.

- Apply colors repeatedly - Use accent shades consistently in all spaces.

- Establish a neutral foundation - Tie rooms together with shared neutral walls/floors.

- Echo colors in textiles - Use pillows, rugs, drapes in palette colors.

- Incorporate corresponding patterns - Unify rooms with matching geometric or floral prints.

- Maximize matching metals & woods - Repeat brass, blackened steel, walnut throughout.

- Coordinate accessories consistently - Use matching vases, trays, candlesholders.

With a harmonious color story guiding décor choices, you grant yourself the freedom to incorporate meaningful memorabilia, vivid artwork, and treasured antiques while still maintaining a feeling of zen and harmony.

Ways to expertly apply a cohesive color palette:

- Paint architectural details - Use accent colors on moldings, ceilings, interior doors.

- Tie together adjacent rooms - Paint adjoining walls shared hues or hang coordinated art.

- Establish bright focal points - Paint indoor entry doors bold accent colors.

- Create colorblocking - Use different brights in blocks on gallery walls.

- Add vibrant window dressings - Hang patterned drapes in signature shades.

- Welcome guests with color - Paint front doors energizing hues.

- Define separate zones - Use different palette colors in each family member's lounge area.

While some spaces like bedrooms cater to individual preferences, upholding one refined palette between public living areas and entryways creates a welcoming flow.

With abundant vibrant hues, thoughtful repetition is key. Echo colors in slipcovered dining chairs, accent pillows, foyer rugs, and art to prevent disjointed rainbow rooms. Aim for purposeful splashes of color not chaotic explosions.

Of course, as seasons and moods change, feel free to rotate accent pieces in new corresponding colors if original hues no longer spark joy. Just maintain a few key signature shades as the common thread.

If particular palette colors hold deep nostalgic meaning, describe their significance to guests. For example, sunshine yellow kitchen walls represent the color of your grandmother's home. This personal symbolism makes the color especially uplifting.

While some spaces work best in conservative, neutral palettes, don't fear vibrant color. Thoughtfully united colors invigorate the spirit. Just take care to apply accent shades judiciously in highlighting doses so they dazzle rather than overwhelm.

Soon your signature palette will provide that crucial feeling of home. Walking in the front door, you'll breathe a contented sigh as surrounding signature colors wash over you like a warm embrace.

Achieving balance between nostalgia and minimalism

For some, rooms brimming with sentimental keepsakes may feel cluttered or overwhelming. When embracing nostalgic dopamine decor, aim to strike a harmonious balance with edited minimalism.

Display your most treasured memorabilia, but with plenty of breather space. Follow these tips:

- Limit frame clusters to special accent walls. Keep remaining walls streamlined.

- Showcase collections and photos within framed shadowboxes for contained displays.

- Arrange sentimental displays in neat groupings rather than scattering pieces randomly.

- Hang a few meaningful pieces of art rather than overloading walls.

- Keep surfaces like mantels and tabletops minimally decorated, changing pieces seasonally.

- Store the bulk of your memorabilia edited out of rotation. Cycle special items in and out.

- Choose sleek frames and display vessels to contrast with personal relics.

- Incorporate nostalgic elements thoughtfully into neutral, modern spaces instead of overly-ornate retro rooms.

- Uphold organization - Use matching boxes, albums, and containers to neatly store cherished items not on display.

While dopamine décor celebrates sentimentality, restraint is needed to prevent spaces from feeling dark, cluttered, or suffocating. The goal is uplifting reminiscence, not hoarding.

When curating memorabilia vignettes:

1. Edit pieces to only your most emotionally uplifting relics. Cherish through minimalism.
2. Arrange displays with plenty of negative space around and between pieces.
3. Limit grouping to intentional tableaus rather than overwhelming entire rooms.
4. Choose sleek vessels like frames and shadowboxes to corral pieces.
5. Showcase memorabilia against neutral backdrops for balance.
6. Rotate extras in and out of storage to refresh displays seasonally.

The combination of pared-back neutral foundations with pops of vibrant color, playful textures, and meaningful memorabilia strikes an ideal balance. You control the nostalgia-to-minimalism ratio depending on your comfort level.

While your home should indeed surround you with cherished keepsakes, the space still requires room to breathe, move and evolve. Cluttered rooms with dark colors can drag mood down. Bright, edited spaces allow your collections to shine.

For most uplifting results, reminisce through a refined lens. Limit sentimental styles like chintz florals, ornate frames, frilly accents. Instead, honor special relics by choosing clean-lined vessels like floating ledge shelves, geometric shadowboxes, and sleek metal frames. This keeps the focus on the irreplaceable personal pieces themselves.

Your home should spotlight the people, places, interests, and values making you who you are - but with care not to overwhelm. Thoughtfully curate and display your most precious memorabilia against a flexible backdrop embracing both beloved collections and wide open spaces.

Preserving Order Within Fullness

While richly layered dopamine decor revels in abundance, restraint is required to prevent our spaces from becoming cluttered and overwhelming havens of hoarding.

Embrace edited maximalism by upholding mindful organization strategies allowing each treasured piece room to shine.

Here are ways to inject spaciousness while making the most of your décor:

- Limit furniture to only essential, multipurpose pieces. Choose designs accommodating integrated storage like coffee tables with lift tops revealing interior shelf storage or benches with cubbies inside.

- Stick to one or two statement pieces per room. Allow substantial empty space around furnishings. For example, rather than filling a living room with multiple armchairs, loveseats and ottomans, choose one fabulous vintage sofa as the seating centerpiece.

- Arrange furniture asymmetrically rather than pushed against walls. Float pieces thoughtfully throughout the middle of a space to keep the center open. Allow ample walkways for traffic flow.

- Build ample shelving and cabinets to stow items when not in use. Conceal clutter in storage ottomans, baskets under console tables, or cabinets so rooms feel peaceful even when packed with possessions.

- Use neutral wall colors and flooring as palate cleansers between vibrant décor. For example, balance a wildly colorful rug with crisp white walls and natural wood flooring. The neutrals prevent visual chaos.

- Showcase collections and memorabilia in neatly organized displays rather than scattered haphazardly. Contain pieces within frames, shadowboxes, shelves, and cabinets thoughtfully.

- For open floor plans, zone spaces through color, lighting and rugs rather than permanent dividers. Keep sightlines open. Define a reading nook within a living room through a vibrant rug, shelving and chair grouping rather than building walls.

● Make the most of vertical space through tall shelving and wall displays. Get visual weight off floors. Fill your walls with gallery photo collages, floating shelves, mounted cabinets and floor-to-ceiling bookcases.

● Incorporate mirrors and reflective accents to create the illusion of more space. Hang an oversized mirrored piece behind your sofa or choose a glass-topped coffee table to make rooms feel airier.

● Take a minimalist approach to surfaces like console tables, mantels and nightstands. Keep them highly edited with just a couple treasured accents on each. Too many objects clustered together appears messy.

● Use multipurpose furniture like storage ottomans and coffee tables to add function. Nest occasional tables like nesting side tables and cubes near seating areas to save space when not in use.

While dopamine decor grants you permission to fully embrace your passions through surrounding yourself with meaningful memorabilia, collections, vivid colors, and playful prints, upholding organization prevents spaces from becoming overwhelming. Make room to breathe.

Aim to create a sense of curation rather than accumulation. Thoughtfully edited abundance and artful disorder that appears intentional is key. Avoid a hurried, random cluttered look.

When arranging your home:

1. Group like items together in neat collection. Contain them within frames, boxes, or displays. For example, gather all coral specimens in a single shadowbox rather than scattering them.
2. Choose storage furnishings that hide items when not in use like trunks, cabinets, and shelving units with doors. Tuck away off-season decor or items that would cause clutter if left out.
3. For collections, rotate pieces in and out seasonally so they don't accumulate chaotically over time. Swap beach shells for snow globes when the seasons change.
4. Prevent flat surfaces from becoming cluttered catchalls. Keep only a few curated accessories and objects in each area. Too many items compete visually.
5. Use calm wall colors as neutral backdrops so vivid pieces pop rather than compete. For example, paint a bookshelf backing a vibrant scarf display a solid neutral tone.
6. Incorporate large statement pieces sparingly. Allow substantial negative space around and between furnishings. Avoid crowding rooms by cramming in too many imposing furnishing pieces.

The beauty of dopamine decor is fully surrounding yourself with things that make your spirit soar. But focus on quality over quantity. Cultivate a curated gallery of your most uplifting items displayed artfully. A touch of restraint preserves the magic.

Strategic Storage Solutions

Creative storage solutions allow you to keep your beloved items nearby without creating clutter. Some ideas include:

- Repurpose furniture intended for other uses like vintage luggage, crates, and toolboxes into holders of treasured objects.

- For media like books, records, movies or games, incorporate custom built-in bookshelves or cabinetry to neatly contain collections.

- Use decorative trunks and chests at the foot of beds or in entryways to hide blankets, linens, and off-season clothing.

- Under-bed storage bins and closet organization systems keep overflow tucked away neatly while remaining accessible.

- For surfaces prone to collecting clutter like dressers, sideboards, and console tables, woven baskets or bins work better than leaving items loose.

- Clear acrylic organizational boxes become invisible ways to neatly corral accessories and supplies in drawers and cabinets.

- Wall mounted rails, hooks, and floating shelves keep frequently used items displayed while freeing up precious floor and surfacespace.

- Cubbies, wall pockets, magazine files and letter sorters affix to walls in offices, kitchens, mudrooms and more to organize loose papers and supplies.

The key is ensuring that every beloved item has a designated storage spot to retreat to when not in use. Concealing away excess rather than allowing clutter to take over rooms is essential.

Creative Storage & Organization Ideas

Here are additional clever storage and organization solutions to consider:

Kitchens:

- Mount pots and pans on walls or from ceilings with racks.

- Store oils and vinegars in countertop carousels for easy access.

- Use sliding drawers for spices so you can see contents easily.

- Keep dishware organized in vertically tiered plate racks.

- Incorporate pull-out waste bin cabinets for separating recycling.

Bedrooms:

- Install under-bed pull out drawers for maximizing hidden storage real estate.

- Use a valet rod and adjustable shelves inside closets for clothing organization.

- Choose a storage bed with built-in drawers under the base.

- Attach a fabric magazine file to the wall beside your nightstand to corral loose papers.

- Use decorative bins and baskets to organize items inside dresser drawers.

Entryways:

- Mount a family command center bulletin board for reminders, mail, and schedules.

- Use wall hooks to hang coats, hats, pet leashes, reusable bags and umbrellas.

- Place a trunk or cabinet with doors to conceal clutter you don't want on display.

- Add a shelf with cubbies for sorting incoming items immediately upon arriving home.

- Use woven baskets to stash shoes and accessories rather than leaving them loose on floors.

Offices:

- Install floating wall shelves at staggered heights for storing supplies within eyesight.

- Use acrylic desktop organizers and trays to corral writing tools in orderly compartments.

- Place a letter sorter on your desk or wall to keep mail and paperwork separated by type.

- Mount wall file sorters with colored labels to neatly contain important documents or project papers.

The key is ensuring that every beloved item has a designated storage spot to retreat to when not in use. Concealing away excess rather than allowing clutter to take over rooms is essential.

Concealing Clutter While Keeping Items Accessible

Clutter easily accumulates simply through living. Rather than strictly purging your belongings, use savvy storage solutions that keep overflow tucked out of sight but still conveniently accessible as needed.

Some tidy storage strategies include:

- Baskets tucked into open console table shelving corral loose items out of sight while keeping them easily accessible in one spot.

- Sturdy acrylic organizers inside drawers neatly contain supplies and smaller items so you can still see what's inside at a glance.

- Fabric poufs on the floor not only serve as extra seating but open up to reveal hidden interior storage.

- Woven floor baskets slipped under accent chairs or tables become invisible catchalls for blankets, remotes or books when company comes over.

- Floating wall ledges mounted a few inches from the wall create a slender surface area to place decor while concealing cords and power strips behind them.

- Metal wall files with suspensions rods allow you to neatly hang folders of paperwork above your workspace to clear off desktops.

- Slide rattan bins under beds to stow extra linens and pillows ordinarily piled on mattresses. The containers maintain order while keeping items handy.

- Purchase coffee tables, ottomans, and beds with lift-tops that open to reveal interior organizing compartments to stash items away neatly.

Take advantage of the vertical dimension to mount ledges, shelves, racks and files that allow you to neatly stow items overhead without sacrificing floorspace. The goal is keeping every belonging in an assigned spot when not in use. Just be sure to label storage bins and shelves so you remember what contents live where!

Strategic Multipurpose Furnishings

Another way to pare down clutter is selecting furnishings that multitask, such as:

- Tufted ottomans with internal storage space for tucking away blankets.

- Wooden trunks that can serve as coffee tables when closed or store linens when open.

- Console tables with built-in cabinets or cubbies for sorting mail and papers.

- Coffee tables and side tables with shelves underneath to hold baskets corralling remotes, chargers and more.

- Floor cushions that flip over to become useful side tables in between uses.

- Nesting side tables like stackable cubes that slide under each other when not in use.

- Upholstered benches that provide seating but lift up to reveal interior toy storage for kids' rooms.

- Desks with a drop-down front that can be folded down to function as a laptop workstation or folded up to be a credenza.

By selecting furniture that serves more than one purpose, you gain function while eliminating the need for additional pieces that contribute clutter. Measure the dimensions of your space carefully when furnishing to confirm that multipurpose pieces will actually fit while fulfilling both roles. But when executed thoughtfully, choose furnishings with bonus uses beyond their primary purpose can allow you to do more with less.

Maintaining Open Floor Plans

For homes embracing more modern open concept architecture, beware overcrowding great rooms and communal spaces with permanent architectural dividers. Here are tips for delineating functional zones without cluttering the openness:

• Define spaces through area rugs in contrasting colors, patterns or materials from the main flooring. The rugs designate sitting, kitchen or dining spaces.

• Angle furniture arrangements toward each other or perpendicular to walls rather than lining everything up flush against perimeter walls, which feels stiff.

• Incorporate distinctive lighting fixtures over key areas like pendant lamps over a kitchen island or table task lamps beside seating areas to differentiate functions.

• Arrange same-purpose furniture into logical groupings rather than scattering pieces aimlessly throughout. For example, float sofas and chairs together to create a clear conversation area.

• Use shelving, screens, or transparent drapes to create separation between spaces while allowing light and sightlines to permeate through open areas.

• Position floor plants and partitions to help divide the space into primary zones. For example, place a storage cabinet between entry and living spaces.

• Maintain open sightlines through doorways, ceilings and windows.

While dopamine decor embraces eclectic richness, too much visual clutter competes for attention in open formats. Uphold strategic organization to prevent cacophony.

Thoughtfully Layering in meaningful Accents

While simplicity can feel sparse, an overabundance of accents also easily overwhelms. When decorating with abundance, thoughtfully layer in accents using these principles:

• Vignettes - Cluster colorful objects into cohesive still life vignettes like coral pieces in a glass cloche display rather than scattering items randomly.

• Rule of Three - Style accents in visually pleasing arrangements of three. For example, three marbles prints over a sofa rather than sprinkling art haphazardly.

• Containment - Use frames, cases and vessels to display themed objects together neatly like showcasing all your seashells in one shadowbox frame.

● Rotation - Swap out accent pieces regularly to refresh your space and rediscover forgotten treasures. Avoid overwhelming stagnant permanent displays.

● Negative Space - Allow substantial breathing room around and between accent groupings. Avoid overly cluttering surfaces and shelves.

● Overhead Storage - Use vertical space for displays. Mount floating shelves, wall cabinets, and racks to clear surfaces.

While dopamine decor celebrates collections and meaningful keepsakes, uphold balance. Cluster special objects in intentionally styled vignettes. Allow each piece and collection room to shine before your eyes and mind.

Edited Maximalism

The beauty of dopamine décor is fully surrounding yourself with things that make your spirit soar. But focus on quality over quantity. Cultivate a curated gallery of your most uplifting items displayed artfully.

Aim for edited maximalism - abundant in treasures that spark joy, but orderly so that each cherished piece can be appreciated individually. Give every book, keepsake, and accessory a permanent displayed home or storage spot.

Upholding organization allows your vibrant décor to feel consciously composed rather than haphazardly accumulated. Displays should convey purposeful personality, not mindless excess.

Preserve the magic through edited abundance. With a touch of restraint, your home transforms into a living sanctuary where you feel centered, inspired, and authentically nurtured.

Final Thoughts on Surrounding Yourself with Joy

If you've made it to this final chapter, you now possess everything you need to infuse your home with happiness by embracing the spirit of dopamine decor. You understand how surrounding yourself with purposeful colors, nostalgic keepsakes, cozy textures, and meaningful memorabilia can uplift your spirit and promote wellbeing.

While trends will come and go, the tips within this book focus on timeless principles of crafting spaces that reflect the unique light within you. Your home provides a sanctuary where you are free to unapologetically celebrate your passions, interests, loves and quirks through symbolic décor.

Remember, dopamine decorating grants you full permission to:

- Paint your walls in colors that lift your mood, evoke beloved memories, and bring you energy. Choose hues that make your soul sing.

- Incorporate playful patterns and prints, from polka dots to preppy plaids, that prompt smiles. Pattern boosts mood.

- Display cherished photos, souvenirs, childhood mementos, and heirlooms proudly. Surround yourself with nostalgia.

- Showcase any collections and treasures that speak to your interests proudly. Let your displayed objects tell your story.

- mix timeless natural textures like wood, rattan, ceramic, and cozy textiles abundantly to create warmth.

- Blend styles fearlessly - modern and antique, sleek and ornate, maximalist and minimalist. The blend reflects you.

- Ignore trends and decorating "rules." Let colors, furnishings, and decor that make you happiest guide all choices.

While some home aesthetics aim for universal appeal, dopamine décor champions self-expression and personal resonance above all else. Surround yourself with pieces imbued with positive memories, radiating welcoming energy, and reflecting your spirit.

Of course, with great décor freedom comes great responsibility. Artful arrangement and thoughtful restraint keep whimsical spaces from becoming overwhelming. We touched on organization strategies like:

1. Upholding cohesive color palettes to tie eclectic spaces together
2. Striking a balance between minimalism and nostalgic keepsakes
3. Containing treasured collections within frames and displays
4. Allowing breathing room around and between furnishings
5. Layering in sentimental memorabilia judiciously against neutral backdrops

The goal is crafting a personalized haven that feels curated, not cluttered. Edit abundance with care.

As you move forward, don't let decorating become a point of stress or perfectionism. Simply build your home gradually, adding special finds over time that make your day brighter. Start small with a cheerful accent wall or collection of nostalgic framed photos.

Above all, listen to your inherent sense of wonder and play. Allow your living space to showcase your inner child while representing the adult you've become. Let go of outside opinions. Decorate unapologetically according to what brings you joy, serenity, inspiration, or comfort.

Remember, a home filled with pieces imbued with personal significance, favorite colors, and meaningful memorabilia is a happy home. Your dwellings are meant to replenish you, not impress others.

Wishing you a future brimming with playful decorating adventures! May the tips within this book guide you to create havens as unique and vibrant as your spirit. Moving forward, listen to your intuition and lean into displays that resonate most with your inner light.

You now hold the blueprint for surrounding yourself with uplifting décor allowing you to live happily, authentically, and unapologetically as your best self each day. Embrace the freedom to decorate distinctly.

Whenever you need inspiration, return to the permission granted within these pages: to craft joyful spaces reflecting the color, whimsy, comfort, and meaning that sings to your soul. Create a sanctuary where you feel free to be yourself.

You've got this! Wishing you profound peace and daily happiness in the haven you cultivate.

Bonus 1 : Dopamine Nation Analysis And Key Learning

The neuroscience behind pleasure and addiction

In her pivotal book "Dopamine Nation," psychiatrist Dr. Anna Lembke illuminates the neuroscience underlying our brain's complex pleasure and reward circuitry. She explains how the neurotransmitter dopamine governs how we experience gratification.

When we bite into a fudgy ganache-filled bonbon, slide into a warm bath, or get a promotion at work, our dopamine levels spike, signaling reward. Our brains catalogue these feel-good activities, reinforcing behaviors that release more happy chemicals.

But just like building up any tolerance, we soon need more sugar, soaks, and success to get the same rush. Our receptors desensitize to once-pleasurable things. Normal joys fade into humdrum habit, driving us to seek bigger thrills to rouse our dampened dopamine response.

In today's era of endless on-demand stimulation, we're constantly bombarded with hyper-rewarding inputs deliberately designed to hijack our feel-good reward circuitry. Junk food, drugs, social media, porn, shopping splurges - all provide supra-normal stimuli engineered to cause surging dopamine release. But what goes up must come down. Each fleeting high gives way to a rebound crash as our neurotransmitters recalibrate. Yet we soon crave another hit to quell the unease. And so the vicious cycle continues.

This phenomenon of hedonic adaptation explains why we end up numbed to pleasures that once delighted us. Our insatiable brains keep demanding ever-greater thrills merely to capture prior levels of satisfaction. But this dopamine-depleting arms race leaves us depleted, depressed, and continually wanting more.

The Dopamine Seeking Cycle

To understand hedonic adaptation, let's break down the vicious dopamine-seeking cycle:

● We partake in an activity known to trigger a dopamine rush and sense of pleasure, such as eating decadent sweets or winning at slots in a casino.

- Our brain registers rapid dopamine spikes signaling reward and catalogs the behavior prompting this response. A feedback loop forms associating the activity with pleasure.

- Overtime as the once-enjoyable activity becomes routine habit, our dopamine receptors downregulate in response to repeated stimulation, becoming numbed and less reactive.

- We now need increased levels of the activity, such as more sugary treats or bigger casino bets, simply to prompt the same moderate dopamine response we once got from a small amount.

- As the cycle escalates, we experience reduced pleasure and reward from habitual behaviors that formerly delighted us. This drives us to seek bigger dopamine spikes from new thrilling behaviors.

- Our appetite for novelty and intensity increases as we begin needing more extreme stimuli to overcome our desensitized neurological reward pathways.

What once registered as a marked dopamine boost now barely registers at all. We're left in deficit, craving artificial highs just to regain baseline satisfaction. The vicious cycle continues.

This diminished sensitivity helps explain why people develop tolerance to pleasures or need to continually up their dopamine-releasing behaviors. Our brains adapt to expect unreasonable levels of stimuli.

Hedonic Adaptation

The tendency to quickly return to a relatively stable level of happiness after positive or negative events is called hedonic adaptation. Essentially we become desensitized to new circumstances alarmingly fast.

For example, buying a fancy new car brings an initial thrill. But a few months later, the buzz of novelty wears off. We adjust to the upgrade as the new normal. The car still runs perfectly but provides less joy. Our brain pushes us to seek fresh highs.

This is the hedonic treadmill - the unsatisfying push for the next dopamine spike. Our set point keeps recalibrating as we adapt to new pleasures and thrills. Making sustainable contentment challenging.

The examples are endless: the shiny gadget stops exciting us after a while, the scenic vacation now feels mundane so we start planning the next getaway before this one ends, the promotion and raise feel lackluster once the initial celebration ends.

While adaptation and habituation serve survival purposes, making us alert to new threats and opportunities, it also prevents us from fully enjoying life's steady joys when reckless novelty-chasing becomes compulsive habit.

Addictive Behaviors and Dopamine

What drives addictive behaviors? Neurologically it comes down to dopamine. When our brains are flooded with rewarding feel-good neurotransmitters, it conditions us to repeat and even chase that short-lived chemical high.

This is why highly pleasurable and stimulating activities pose risk of becoming unhealthy compulsions. Our reward system drives us to recreate the same flood of feel-good brain chemicals.

Let's examine how dopamine fuels different forms of addiction:

Drug and Alcohol Addiction

- Psychoactive substances directly trigger surging dopamine release and activation of associated reward pathways. With repeated exposure, the brain downregulates receptors to compensate, requiring more and more of the substance just to achieve baseline.

Food Addiction

- Hyper-palatable foods like sugar and fat light up reward pathways. The more excessively we eat, the more dopamine receptors gets blunted over time, driving us to seek further indulgence and ever-intensifying flavors and quantities.

Shopping/Spending Addiction

- Scoring great deals floods the brain with "retail therapy" dopamine. Over time, shoppers may need to make riskier splurges and purchases simply to achieve the same joy and validation.

Pornography Addiction

- Viewing pornography spikes dopamine along with oxytocin and endorphins, creating a short-term but powerful neurochemical high and sense of escape that leaves viewers wanting more once the comedown arrives.

Gambling Addiction

- The unpredictability of wins lights up dopamine pathways connected to reward and motivation. Even as the craving for higher stakes and more bets increases, diminished returns leave us chasing ever-elusive jackpots.

Social Media Addiction

- Scrolling offers intermittent mini-dopamine bursts in anticipation of what we might discover next. When platform algorithms serve up variable rewards, it hooks our habit-forming reward system.

In summary, when pleasurable shortcuts hijack healthy dopamine reward modulation, it can spiral into destructive addictive behaviors that narrowly fixate on chasing the next superficial high. Our depth of fulfillment diminishes even as our thirst for quick-hit novelty and intensity deepens.

Impacts of Dopamine Dependence

What goes up must come down. When dopamine gets depleted through constant artificial over-stimulation, we experience:

- Anhedonia - inability to feel pleasure from normally enjoyable activities

- Dysphoria - feelings of unease, instability and dissatisfaction

- Depression and anxiety - chronic low mood and worry

- Fatigue - pleasure-seeking and withdrawal is physically and mentally exhausting

- Increased stress reactivity - less resilience in the face of challenges

- Compulsivity - obsessive pursuit of dopamine boosts

- Diminished focus - attention gets splintered by cravings and unease

- Reduced motivation - everyday responsibilities lose appeal

- Weakened willpower and self-discipline

- Shame, secrecy, and isolation - addiction breeds hiding and dishonesty

Essentially, the more we artificially stimulate feel-good neurotransmitter pathways, the more dysregulated our stress and reward systems become. We end up in a deficit state, needing constant dopamine just to bring us to baseline. This instability and unease fuels addictive tendencies.

Dopamine Dysregulation

What underlies dopamine dysregulation? There are myriad factors at play:

- Genetic - Variations in dopamine reception and metabolic genes affect signaling and influence addiction vulnerability.

- Environmental - Highly stimulating inputs and chronic stressors tax dopamine reserves and receptors.

- Trauma - Early emotional, physical or psychological trauma is strongly correlated to adult addiction tendencies.

- Mental Health - Mood disorders, anxiety, ADHD, and schizophrenia involve disrupted dopamine modulation.

- Physical Health - Obesity, chronic inflammation, gut health, sleep disorders, and hormonal imbalances impact dopamine.

- Personality - Impulsivity, novelty-seeking, and extraversion are tied to greater dopamine-reward drives.

In essence, dopamine signaling disruptions stem from complex gene-environment interactions. There are often multi-faceted physiological and psychological factors at play driving compulsive addiction-prone behaviors. Quick fixes fail to address root causes.

Holistic Addiction Treatment

According to Lembke, simply eliminating addictive substances or behaviors often proves ineffectual if underlying issues remain unresolved. Without addressing deep-seated trauma, mental health struggles, or genetic and environmental factors, the addiction whack-a-mole continues. Recovery requires holistic treatment of the whole person, inside and out.

Comprehensive treatment should encompass:

- Psychotherapy to address cognitive distortions and underlying emotional issues

- Medication assisted treatment to stabilize brain chemistry

- Nutritional optimization to support mental health

- Physical fitness regimens to stimulate feel-good neurochemicals

- CBT and mindfulness to build distress tolerance

- Support groups to overcome isolation and shame

- Nature immersion for perspective and dopamine modulation

- Meaningful social connection and community belonging

- Stress management and health work-life balance

- Developing emotional intelligence and communication skills

The goal is healing the brain and teaching healthy coping strategies while also approaching the environmental, social, and lifestyle factors that feed into addictive tendencies holistically. Sustainability comes from lifestyle change.

Dopamine Detoxing

Along with professional treatment plans, "dopamine detoxing" has gained popularity as a self-help technique aimed at resetting overstimulated reward systems by:

- Avoiding highly stimulating and dopamine-triggering foods, drugs, behaviors

- Practicing mindfulness, deep breathing, meditation, and yoga

- Spending time in nature away from screens and devices

- Allowing boredom instead of constantly chasing external stimulation

- Partaking in creative activities rather than passive consumption

- Engaging in human connection versus digital socializing

- Replacing quick dopamine hits with healthier sustainable feel-good practices

The idea is that by giving the brain a break from constant hyper-stimulation, receptors can reset and return to homeostasis, restoring sensitivity to simpler joys and healthier motivations. Play, not escapism, is the goal.

Recalibrating Your Joy Meter

According to Lembke, to counteract this endless drive for the next short-lived high, we must recalibrate our reward system by swapping quick fixes for more mindful joys. Meditation, exercise, immersion in nature, and meaningful social connections may stimulate less intense dopamine spikes, but their benefits compound and endure. When we reset our hedonic set point and savor simpler pleasures, cravings for constant empty novelty subside. We discover fulfillment in stillness.

Here are science-backed practices that stimulate sustainable dopamine for wellbeing:

Cardiovascular Exercise

- Aerobic activity prompts a gentle rush of dopamine along with endorphins, lowering stress and boosting motivation for tasks ahead. The benefits accumulate over time through consistency.

Creative Projects

- Immersing yourself in hands-on hobbies like gardening, baking, painting, or DIY projects provides small ongoing micro-bursts of pride and dopamine with each incremental step forward.

Meditation

- Calming practices heighten dopamine signaling to the brain's prefrontal cortex responsible for executive functioning, focus, and judgment. Mental clarity increases.

Generosity

- Helping others in need provides a genuine "helper's high" through dopamine and serotonin release, along with renewed meaning and connection.

Human Touch

● Hugging friends and family, cuddling pets, sensual intimacy, affectionate touch and skin-to-skin contact all trigger oxytocin and dopamine elevations that combat isolation.

Gratitude

● Regularly expressing genuine thankfulness lights up dopamine pathways tied to benefit and reward. Keeping a gratitude journal rewires your brain's motivation response.

Learning

● Seeking out knowledge provides micro-bursts of dopamine with each new neural connection formed. Memory retention boosts self-efficacy.

So in decorating and in life, seek balance. Limit aimless dopamine-chasing and make space for reflection. Cherish nostalgia's sweetness but don't become stuck chasing the past. Combine beloved collections with optimistic future visions. Design comfortable sanctuaries and also wide-open spaces that invite fresh possibility. Look beyond the quick hit to find beauty in subtle, lasting joys that nourish your spirit every day.

8 Key Takeaways To Be Applied Daily:

1. **Understand the Role of Dopamine:** Dopamine is a neurotransmitter responsible for the feeling of pleasure and reward. Overexposure to stimuli that cause dopamine surges can lead to decreased sensitivity and increased craving for more intense experiences.

1. **Recognize the Influence of Modern Society:** We live in a society saturated with highly pleasurable and addictive stimuli like fast food, drugs, social media, and pornography. These stimuli can hijack our reward system and create a cycle of overindulgence and addiction.

1. **Adopt a Holistic Approach to Addiction:** Addiction is a complex issue influenced by various factors, including genetics, childhood experiences, and social environment. Addressing addiction requires a comprehensive approach that considers the individual's whole life.

1. **Practice Hedonic Recalibration:** Rebalance your brain's reward system by reducing exposure to highly pleasurable and addictive stimuli. Replace these with activities that provide more sustainable and meaningful sources of pleasure, such as exercise, meditation, and social connections.

1. **Mindfulness and Self-Reflection:** Practice mindfulness and self-reflection to develop a healthier relationship with pleasure and reward. Recognize your triggers and vulnerabilities and develop strategies to manage them effectively.

1. **Prioritize Relationships:** Cultivate meaningful social connections, as they play a crucial role in maintaining mental health and well-being. Strong relationships can provide a source of support, fulfillment, and pleasure that is more sustainable and healthy than artificial stimuli.

1. **Embrace a Balanced Lifestyle:** Adopt a balanced and sustainable approach to pleasure and reward. This includes re-evaluating the role of technology and social media in your life, promoting healthier lifestyles, and creating an environment that prioritizes mental health and well-being.

1. **Gratitude and Acceptance:** Practice gratitude for the small and simple pleasures in life. Accept that pain and discomfort are natural parts of life and that seeking constant pleasure

and reward can lead to imbalance and addiction.

Bonus 2: Dopamine Detox

Understanding Dopamine

Dopamine is one of our brain's crucial neurotransmitters, playing a central role in motivation, focus, and feelings of pleasure and reward. When dopamine levels spike, we experience that delightful rush signaling our brain to repeat enjoyable activities. From savoring a gooey dessert to getting a promotion at work, dopamine provides that little burst of satisfaction when we do something rewarding.

But problems arise when our reward circuitry gets overstimulated. In today's world of endless on-demand indulgences like junk food, drugs, social media, porn, and online shopping, our brains are constantly bombarded with dopamine-releasing stimuli. With overexposure, our dopamine receptors start to downregulate, becoming less responsive to everyday pleasures.

We begin needing bigger and better hits just to register the same level of enjoyment. A single scoop of ice cream stops satisfying us, so we devour the whole pint tub to recapture that initial dopamine delight. Social media likes that once thrilled us start feeling meaningless without an endless stream of notifications. This phenomenon is called hedonic adaptation - our baseline happiness keeps ratcheting up, demanding ever stronger inputs to reach the same rewarding feeling.

This insatiable drive for novelty and intensity leaves us stuck on a dopamine-depleting hamster wheel, seeking our next fix but finding less fulfillment. Our overstimulated receptors numb us to the small wonders already surrounding us. The rose loses its scent.

To break this vicious cycle of chasing bigger highs, we need to reset our dopamine levels and resensitize our reward circuitry. Enter: the dopamine detox.

What is Dopamine Detox

The concept of a "dopamine detox" has gained popularity as a way to temporarily cut back on dopamine-triggering stimuli and allow your brain's receptors to recalibrate. The premise is straightforward: by taking a break from intensely pleasurable indulgences, you can renew sensitivity to more subtle joys and break free of dependency on novelty and excess.

A dopamine detox essentially involves:

- Limiting exposure to hyper-stimulating activities and inputs

- Choosing simpler, more mindful pleasures instead

- Giving your dopamine receptors a chance to reset and recover

By avoiding addictive behaviors and stimuli for a period of time - say a weekend or a week - proponents believe you can hit the reset button on your brain's reward system. This may help restore a baseline happiness set point so you regain appreciation for ordinary pleasures often drowned out by overstimulation.

Detoxing from Dopamine-Triggering Activities

What does refraining from intense dopamine hits look like in practice? Here are some activities to temporarily limit during a detox:

- Binging hyper-palatable foods like sugar, salt and junk food

- Marathon gaming, TV, YouTube or porn sessions

- Doomscrolling social media feeds for hours

- Online shopping binges for instant gratification

- Compulsively checking texts, emails, alerts for fresh notifications

- Gambling, whether online or in casinos

- Binge drinking or recreational drug use

- Endlessly surfing the web and clicking links

- Letting Spotify autoplay song after song

- Mindlessly snacking out of boredom

The key is to temporarily restrict behaviors that have become compulsive dopamine-chasing habits. Don't totally deprive yourself, but consciously set defined limits on activities prone to overindulgence.

Practicing Mindful Pleasures Instead

Instead of seeking constant highs, devote your time to more mindful activities like:

- Going for walks outdoors without your phone

- Reading books or listening to podcasts

- Creative hobbies like drawing, playing music

- Socializing with friends and family without distractions

- Cooking and eating nutritious whole foods

- Exercising, stretching and meditating

- Completing pending tasks and chores

- Journaling and quiet reflection

- Engaging with art, nature or your community

- Practicing full presence during daily experiences

The goal isn't to deprive yourself or create suffering. It's to trade quick dopamine rushes for slower-burning satisfactions. By hitting pause on intense stimulation, we rediscover steadier sources of meaning and joy already within us. We rekindle our natural curiosity and capacity for presence.

How Dopamine Detoxing Resets the Brain's Reward System

Let's explore exactly how taking a break from constant overstimulation helps reset your brain's reward pathways:

- Hyper-stimulating behaviors like drug use, gaming, porn, or sugary treats flood the brain with rapid, amplified dopamine spikes.

- In response to the unnaturally intense dopamine rush, the brain downregulates receptors to protect itself, numbing you to the experience.

- The baseline number of available receptors decreases as the brain becomes conditioned to expect this artificial level of stimulation.

- In the absence of the extreme stimulus, available dopamine is now less effective at binding with scarcer receptors, producing a deficit state.

- By removing the intense dopamine influx for a period of time, receptors upregulate and return to equilibrium. Your baseline sensitivity resets.

● Ordinary pleasures and healthy motivating behaviors again trigger normal dopamine spikes, reigniting your reward response. Resensitization occurs!

Essentially, detoxing allows your brain's reward system to normalize after developing tolerance to unhealthy levels of stimulation that left you needing more and more to feel satisfaction.

Tips for an Effective Dopamine Detox

If you want to experiment with a dopamine detox, here are some tips and best practices:

● Set a realistic timeframe - Figure out a manageable period for your detox, like a weekend or a few days free of intense commitments. Extend as feels right.

● Start slowly - Ease into limiting stimuli vs suddenly going cold turkey, which tends to backfire. Taper usage at a steady pace.

● Keep it tech-free - Turn off notifications and remove distracting apps from your homescreen during your detox. Disable autoplays and recommendations to avoid rabbit holes.

● Plan engaging alternatives - Have alternative activities lined up like hikes, books, arts, crafts and organizational projects to fill your time.

● Get support - Enlist friends and family to join your detox or at least understand your need for space. Making your needs known helps garner support.

● Note obstacles - Pay attention to what situations, cues or emotions drive you back to bad habits and work to neutralize those triggers.

● Avoid tempting locations - Steer clear of malls, movie theaters, bars and other hotbeds of indulgence while detoxing.

● Reward yourself - Plan a special outing, meal or treats after your detox time as something to look forward to. Just don't go overboard.

● Focus on additions - Try new hobbies, routines and healthy habits rather than solely focusing on restricting pleasure during your detox period. What can you add to your life?

● Be compassionate - Don't beat yourself up for lapses. Progress happens gradually. Simply reset and return to your detox when needed.

● Customize your approach - Your detox plan will be unique. Adapt as you discover which restrictive and restorative practices work best for you long-term.

A dopamine detox is highly personalized so be flexible. The overall goal remains recalibrating your dopamine response, but the specific plan varies based on your needs and habits.

Potential Benefits of Dopamine Detoxing

While the research on dopamine fasting's effects is limited, many self-report positive outcomes like:

● Increased presence and focus - With less digital noise and distraction demanding attention, focus zeros in on the tangible present moment.

● Renewed appreciation for subtle joys - As extreme stimuli are limited, you regain gratitude for simple pleasures like reading, conversing, or savoring a warm drink. Anhedonia lifts.

● Improved mood and motivation - As your dopamine system resets, you feel more energized to channel motivation into personal priorities that get neglected when you're in a constant quest for quick hits.

● More conscious choices - Away from visceral cravings and impulse, you tap into wisdom to make thoughtful decisions aligned with your wellbeing.

● Healthier habits - With compulsive habits on hold, you naturally gravitate toward more nourishing daily routines that support your mind and body.

● Less anxiety, more calm - Unplugging from the hyper-stimulating modern world quiets the nervous system. You find rest in stillness.

● Renewed creativity - Time away from digital noise and distraction opens space for your innate imagination to flourish as you tinker and play.

By periodically taking a break from overstimulation you restore sensitivity to simpler pleasures while curbing excessive appetite for quick hits of pleasure at any cost. Healthy balance is the goal.

Avoiding Pitfalls of Dopamine Detoxing

To ensure your dopamine detox is productive, avoid these common pitfalls:

● Restricting too severely - Allowing some balanced pleasures keeps the process sustainable. Don't attempt to detox all stimuli at once.

● Depriving yourself - Framing it as self-punishment or penance backfires. The goal is mindful moderation, not suffering. Keep perspective.

● Bouncing back hard - Don't use your detox as an excuse to eventually overindulge. Take it slow when reintroducing stimuli.

● Obsessing about lapses - Progress isn't linear. Guilt helps nothing. Just gently return focus to your detox when distractions arise.

● Deliberately tempting yourself - Don't intentionally dangle risky stimuli if you know you lack restraint. Set yourself up for success.

● Compulsively tracking progress - Don't let measurement become its own distraction. Keep awareness informal.

● Assuming it's a solo cure-all - Detoxing complements treatment and self-work, it doesn't replace it. Use the clarity it provides to build sustainable change.

The point isn't to completely swear off pleasures forever. It's simply taking a temporary break to recalibrate your dopamine response and regain perspective around your habits. Don't put pressure on the process.

Transitioning Back to Balance

After your detox period, avoid immediately rushing back to intense stimuli. Maintain mindful moderation by:

● Slowly reintroducing eliminated activities in limited amounts

● Noticing when cravings creep back in as your use increases

● Keeping the restorative habits and practices you began during your detox

- Carrying your newfound presence and gratitude for subtle joys forward

- Paying closer attention to how certain activities truly make you feel

- Being more selective and intentional with how you use your time and energy

Rather than an unsustainable quick fix, consider a dopamine detox a helpful reset when you've fallen into unhealthy dependency on stimulation. Use the clarity it provides to build more sustainable habits and routines that best nourish you.

The goal of any cleanse should be lasting awareness, not perfection. By periodically challenging your relationship with reward and pleasure, you gain wisdom around your needs and patterns. Resensitize yourself to life's subtle splendors.

Additional Tips for Dopamine Detoxing

Here are some final tips to maximize the benefits of a dopamine detox:

- Tell loved ones - Explain to friends and family that you are doing a digital detox and may be hard to reach. Enlist their support.

- Remove temptations - Delete addictive apps from your devices and hide tempting sugary snacks during your cleanse period.

- Start your day right - Begin each morning of your detox with meditation, affirmations, or yoga to set a mindful tone.

- Plan nutritious meals - Eliminate processed foods and opt for energizing whole food meals and snacks to keep your mood and focus stable.

- Get moving - Supplement screen time with active hobbies like hiking, cleaning, or exercising to lift your natural endorphin and dopamine levels.

- List inspiring goals - Realign with your core aspirations and values. Let these guide your time rather than distraction.

- Keep a journal - Note your emotions, challenges, insights and takeaways from your dopamine detox experience for integration.

By periodically taking a break from potent stimulation, you build mindfulness of your habits and can reset any creeping dependency on external validation, novelty-chasing, and quick hits of pleasure. Create space for quieter joys that sustain you.

Bonus 3 : Dopamine Agonists

Dopamine is an essential neurotransmitter that activates our brain's pleasure and reward circuitry. Agonists are compounds that mimic and boost the effects of neurotransmitters. So dopamine agonists are drugs that bind to dopamine receptors and stimulate them, ramping up dopamine activity in the brain.

By increasing dopamine signaling at the receptor level, these compounds can offer therapeutic benefits related to mood, movement, and neurological conditions. Dopamine agonists provide targeted relief by acting as surrogate keys fitting into the brain's specialized dopamine locks.

When our natural dopamine production declines, sending neural signals awry, dopamine agonists can step in to pick up the slack. Like a boost of revitalizing caffeine for our lagging dopamine systems, these drugs activate feel-good dopaminergic pathways when our own neurotransmitters fall short.

From easing Parkinson's symptoms to stabilizing prolactin levels, the carefully calibrated effects of prescription dopamine agonists allow them to play a powerful role in regulating brain function. Understanding these substances provides insight into how we can harness dopamine's gifts purposefully.

By exploring how synthetic and natural compounds act at receptor sites to augment dopamine neurotransmission, we illuminate the nuanced dynamics between neurotransmitters, receptors, and essential brain processes governing our health and wellbeing. Let's dive deeper!

Exploring the Major Categories of Dopamine Agonists

When our brains' natural dopamine production falls out of harmonious balance, there are several classes of receptor-binding medications we can use to pick up the slack. Let's explore the major categories of dopamine agonists in depth:

Dopamine Precursors

Some of the most widely used dopamine-boosting compounds are amino acid precursors that our bodies readily convert into dopamine itself.

L-DOPA, also known as levodopa, is an especially popular precursor because it easily crosses the blood-brain barrier before getting synthesized into dopamine. Our brains recognize L-DOPA as the raw ingredient for cooking up more of our deficient feel-good neurotransmitter.

Think of taking L-DOPA as analogous to tossing tyrosine, the amino acid building block for dopamine, right into our neurochemical kitchen. Our enzymatic chefs get to work whipping up fresh dopamine molecules.

By increasing levels of dopamine's direct precursor, we can renew depleted reserves of the essential signaling molecule. L-DOPA preparations like Sinemet are therefore standard treatments for dopamine deficiency disorders like Parkinson's disease.

Non-Ergoline Dopamine Receptor Agonists

While precursors aim to increase overall dopamine levels, other agonists directly stimulate dopamine receptors instead. These synthetic compounds activate the receptors without metabolizing into dopamine itself.

Non-ergoline agonists like pramipexole, ropinirole, and rotigotine are chemically unrelated to ergot alkaloids. This differentiated structure allows more targeted receptor binding with fewer side effects compared to ergoline agonists.

Pramipexole (Mirapex) preferentially stimulates the D3 subtype of dopamine receptor and is used for treating Parkinson's and restless leg syndrome. Ropinirole (Requip) has affinity for both D2 and D3 receptors and therefore also aids multiple conditions.

The rotigotine transdermal patch (Neupro) enables continuous dopamine receptor activation by steadily delivering the drug through the skin. This round-the-clock stimulation can smooth out inconsistent symptom relief.

Ergoline-Derived Dopamine Agonists

Ergolines like bromocriptine, cabergoline, and pergolide come from ergot alkaloids, compounds derived from the ergot fungus. While effective receptor binders, they are more likely to cause side effects due to their interaction with additional receptors for other neurotransmitters like serotonin.

Bromocriptine (Parlodel) was the first ergoline agonist approved and is used for treating hormone imbalances like hyperprolactinemia as well as Parkinson's. Cabergoline (Dostinex) has a very long half-life, requiring less frequent dosing.

Lisuride and pergolide were initially popular agonists but became less prescribed due to risk of cardiac valve problems. However, new extended-release preparations aim to provide symptom relief with reduced side effects.

As research on these complex compounds continues, we are discovering safer ways to fine-tune dopamine system functioning. Tailoring dopaminergic therapy to each patient's needs can restore harmony in runaway or deficient neurotransmitter activity.

The Multifaceted Medical Applications of Dopamine Agonists

Dopamine agonists have emerged as frontline treatments for an array of conditions involving dysfunctional dopamine signaling and hormone regulation. Let's dig deeper into some of their major FDA-approved and off-label uses:

Treating Motor Symptoms in Parkinson's Disease

- One of the most well-established uses of dopamine agonists is managing motor symptoms of Parkinson's disease like tremor, rigidity, bradykinesia, and postural instability. Because Parkinson's involves the progressive loss of dopamine-producing neurons in the substantia nigra, directly stimulating dopamine receptors can help compensate for declining dopamine levels and restore smooth motor control.

- Dopamine precursors like levodopa and carbidopa are standards of care for managing Parkinson's symptoms. These oral medications raise dopamine levels in the brain by increasing production. But as neuron degeneration advances, oral dopamine becomes less effective due to reduced storage capacity. This leads to fluctuating symptoms and dyskinesia side effects from uneven dopamine fluctuations.

- As Parkinson's progresses, direct-acting dopamine receptor agonists like pramipexole, ropinirole, rotigotine, apomorphine, and bromocriptine become essential parts of the medication regimen. Since these drugs bypass the presynaptic synthesis stage and directly stimulate postsynaptic dopamine receptors instead, they provide more continuous activation of dopaminergic pathways disrupted in Parkinson's.

- Extended release and controlled release preparations help maintain stable, consistent symptom relief as the drugs achieve longer-lasting therapeutic levels rather than spiking and dropping. Implementing dopamine agonists along with levodopa helps minimize motor complications from wearing-off phenomena over the long-term treatment course.

- Each dopamine agonist possesses slightly different receptor binding profiles, onset and durations of action, and safety considerations, allowing neurologists to customize therapy based on each Parkinson's patient's specific needs and response. While unable to halt disease progression, optimized medication regimens grant motor control and improved quality of life.

Managing Restless Legs Syndrome

- Dopamine agonists offer profound relief for patients with moderate to severe restless legs syndrome (RLS). Pramipexole and ropinirole are FDA-approved as first-line RLS treatments due to their consistent efficacy and favorable side effect profiles.

- These dopamine receptor binding drugs enhance signaling in areas implicated in restless legs syndrome such as the substantia nigra pars compacta and putamen. Studies demonstrate their effectiveness for reducing the core defining RLS symptoms - unpleasant sensations like tingling or itching paired with an uncontrollable urge to move the legs.

- While not fully curative, taken daily at individualized therapeutic dosages, pramipexole and ropinirole can eliminate RLS symptoms for most patients. The dopamine agonists provide dependable relief while avoiding the potential for augmentation and rebound that can occur with repeated intermittent use of sedatives for acute nighttime RLS episodes.

- For severe refractory RLS, injectable dopamine agonists may be implemented, such as subcutaneous apomorphine injections at bedtime to prevent nightly symptoms for 24 hours. While more invasive, injectables enable precise symptom control overnight with minimal daytime sedation or fatigue side effects.

Treating Prolactinomas and Pituitary Tumors

- Dopamine receptor activation in the pituitary gland decreases prolactin secretion from specialized lactotroph cells. Therefore, ergoline-derived dopamine agonists like bromocriptine and cabergoline are highly effective treatments for abnormally elevated prolactin levels caused by prolactinomas and other prolactin-secreting pituitary tumors.

- Hyperprolactinemia leads to a cluster of symptoms including amenorrhea, galactorrhea, hirsutism, reduced bone density, and hypogonadism. By normalizing prolactin through dopamine agonist therapy, these troubling manifestations can be reversed or minimized.

- Dopamine agonists also induce apoptosis and shrink tumor size while suppressing hormone overproduction at the cellular level. Cabergoline is especially useful due to its high receptor affinity, selective pituitary targeting, and long half-life enabling less frequent, convenient dosing. Patients require close monitoring, however, for potential cardiac valve, retinal, and pulmonary fibrosis side effects with long-term usage.

● When used judiciously, dopamine agonists transform prognosis in prolactinoma and pituitary tumor cases from disabling to highly manageable through their targeted anti-prolactin action. Patients regain regular periods, fertility, bone density, and overall wellbeing while tumors reduce in size.

Emerging Uses in Addiction and Neuropsychiatric Disorders

● While not yet FDA-approved, early research indicates dopamine agonists like pramipexole may also benefit disorders like fibromyalgia, treatment-resistant depression, PTSD, tinnitus, addiction recovery, compulsive behaviors, and personality disorders. Their dopamine-elevating effects show promising therapeutic potential for certain neuropsychiatric conditions involving dopamine dysregulation.

● Proposed mechanisms include:

1. Elevating low baseline dopamine implicated in disorders like depression, fatigue and compulsion
2. Stabilizing dopamine signaling made irregular by environmental stressors or trauma
3. Reducing dopamine-related symptoms like anxiety, insomnia, irritability, and poor focus
4. Rebalancing pleasure-reward pathways disrupted by addictive substances
5. Enhancing executive function and impulse control
6. However, more research is still needed to fully elucidate the mechanisms whereby dopamine agonists provide neuropsychiatric relief in humans. Their complex receptor interactions are still being mapped. And risks like increased gambling behaviors require careful consideration when expanding usage clinically.

● But as our understanding of dopamine's nuanced roles deepens through advancing PET scans, genetics, and controlled clinical trials, we are discovering promising new applications for precision-targeted dopamine agonists based on individual neurochemistry. Prescribing practices continue evolving to restore optimal signaling levels and dopaminergic functioning for improved mental health and wellbeing.

The Therapeutic Potential of Apomorphine

Among dopamine receptor agonists, apomorphine possesses unique pharmacodynamic properties that make it especially promising for diverse therapeutic applications:

Parkinson's Disease:

- Provides rapid and reliable relief from episodic motor and non-motor symptoms

- Can rescue patients from "off" states when oral medications are delayed or dyskinetic

- Its speed of onset and short duration enables precise, intermittent dosing right when symptoms flare

Addiction:

- Diminishes opioid and alcohol withdrawal and drug cravings through dopamine stabilization

- Lessens compulsive impulses and addictive behaviors

Depression and Anxiety:

- Has antidepressant, anxiolytic and anti-suicidal effects from dopamine activation

- Fast-acting for quickly alleviating symptoms or panic attacks

- Enhances motivation, sociability and enjoyment

While apomorphine can cause nausea when administered subcutaneously, new delivery methods like sublingual films are improving its tolerability while making use easier. This unique dopamine agonist shows potential for managing both motor and psychiatric conditions through its versatile pharmacology.

Augmentation Therapy in Addiction Recovery

The dopaminergic effects of certain agonists also appear promising for augmentation therapy assisting addiction recovery. While risky in active users, preliminary evidence indicates dopamine agonists may support long-term sobriety when administered under medical supervision by:

- Stabilizing irregular dopamine signaling damaged by chronic substance abuse

- Reducing drug cravings and withdrawal symptoms

- Improving cognitive deficits like poor concentration and judgment

- Lessening compulsive behaviors and impulsivity

- Helping regain healthy motivation, mood, and reward response

By directly modifying dopamine neurotransmission disrupted in addiction, agonists could aid recovery when combined with behavioral interventions, group support, and talk therapy. Preventing relapse by normalizing reward pathways remains an urgent need.

While dopamine alone doesn't "cure" addiction given its psychosocial complexities, strategically enhancing dopaminergic tone shows potential for helping restore neurochemical balance damaged by repeated drug-induced highs and withdrawal lows. Future research will continue clarifying which subgroups could benefit most from dopamine-modulating medications when integrated with holistic treatment programs.

Dopamine Agonists for Fibromyalgia Relief

Fibromyalgia patients experience widespread muscle pain, profound fatigue, insomnia, memory problems and mood disorders. Emerging research hints that dopamine deficiencies in certain brain regions may underlie fibromyalgia's neurological symptoms.

Patients have demonstrated abnormal D2 receptor binding potentials in the striatum, insula, amygdala and other structures compared to healthy controls. This led to studying whether boosting dopamine signaling could offer symptomatic relief.

In open-label trials, the non-ergot agonists pramipexole and ropinirole significantly reduced pain, depression and fatigue severity for a subset of fibromyalgia patients over two months. While not a cure, dopamine modulation improved symptoms and quality of life for many participants. Controlled follow-up studies will further assess efficacy and help identify likely responders versus non-responders.

While mechanisms require clarification, fibromyalgia patients may benefit from dopamine agonists' combined antidepressant, anti-fatigue, anti-pain and pro-motivation properties via neural pathways involved in chronic stress, inflammation and insomnia. Enhancing accountability through medication also improves adherence with exercise and lifestyle changes.

Future Research Directions

Thanks to rapid advancements in PET scanning, functional MRI, genetics, and molecular pharmacology, our understanding of dopamine's nuanced neurological roles deepens each year. Already this has revealed promising new applications for precision-targeted dopamine agonists.

We now appreciate dopamine's diverse functions span far beyond simply promoting movement and reward-seeking. Dopaminergic pathways regulate cognition, motivation, hormonal release, immune activity, mood, sleep, learning, and more.

As researchers elucidate deficiencies underlying specific conditions, we may uncover tailored dopaminergic medications capable of restoring optimal signaling levels and functioning for improved mental health and wellbeing. Already novel dopamine-modulating drugs show potential for once-treatment-resistant conditions.

The applications will only continue expanding as we clarify dopamine's intricate ties to focus, impulse control, social reward, trauma response, resilience, and overall neurological homeostasis. Future discoveries will unlock targeted dopamine agonist therapies for those suffering who cannot wait. This remains an exciting priority in pharmacology, neurology and psychiatry moving forward.

How Dopamine Agonists Exert Their Effects in the Brain

Dopamine agonists provide therapeutic benefit by directly binding to and activating dopamine receptor subtypes, particularly D2 and D3 receptors. Let's unpack their mechanisms of action:

Binding Dopamine Receptors

The basic premise underlying dopamine agonists' effects is that they binds to specific dopamine receptor sites on neurons as an agonist would.

Some like bromocriptine have high affinity for D2 receptors while others like pramipexole preferentially bind D3. When they attach, this stimulates the receptor in the same way that dopamine would, initiating events inside the cell.

Mimicking Dopamine's Actions

By docking directly onto dopamine receptors, agonists mimic the effects of dopamine binding at that site. Their chemical structure allows them to act as dopaminergic signaling molecules.

Essentially, dopamine agonists fool the receptors into thinking they are dopamine. This prompts the same downstream cellular changes, like second messenger system activation, that dopamine triggers.

Boosting Dopamine Signaling

When our brains' dopamine production falters, taking a dopamine agonist can compensate by amplifying signaling at the receptor level.

It's like turning up the volume on a stereo when the power starts running low - the music might be quieter, but boosting the output amplifies the signal. Similarly, agonists enhance dopamine's effects when deficits occur.

This mechanism effectively counteracts conditions involving low dopamine states like Parkinson's disease and restless leg syndrome. By bypassing the need for dopamine release and directly stimulating receptors, agonists boost neurotransmission.

However, in disorders like schizophrenia that involve dopamine excess, antagonists that block receptors may be preferred. The key is rectifying imbalanced signaling.

In essence, dopamine agonists act as molecular mimics of our main "feel good" neurotransmitter. By binding and activating receptors, they can amplify, inhibit, modulate, and fine-tune dopaminergic signaling in nuanced ways. This chemical key-in-lock mechanism powers their therapeutic effects.

Understanding this receptor pharmacology sheds light on how we can precisely adjust neurotransmitter messaging using specially-crafted synthetic and natural compounds. Wielding these tools, we can potentially unlock dopamine's gifts with enhanced precision

The Exciting Frontiers of Dopamine Agonist Research and Drug Development

As our knowledge of dopamine signaling expands, researchers are continually developing promising new dopamine agonists and exploring their potential applications. What does the future of these drugs look like?

Novel Dopamine Agonists

Several next-generation dopamine receptor activators are in the pipeline, including:

- ABT-724 - This highly selective D2 agonist is in Phase 1 trials for treating Parkinson's and restless legs. It aims to provide symptom relief with reduced side effects.

- AZD-1962 - An orally available D2/D3 agonist now in Phase 1b trials for treating Parkinson's symptoms. As a controlled release agent, it may provide smoother, sustained effects.

- STD-101 - A potential first-in-class D1 dopamine receptor selective compound now in preclinical development. Stimulating D1 may enhance neuroplasticity and cognitive function.

- D-512 - A plant-based D2 agonist derived from the alkaloid Annona muricata is in preclinical research for Parkinson's treatment with a lower side effect profile.

These novel agents aim to build upon the success of marketed dopamine agonists by optimizing receptor targeting, drug delivery, and side effect reduction. Developing selective compounds that activate specific dopamine receptor subtypes holds promise for customized treatment.

Treating Addiction

Early research indicates dopamine agonists like pramipexole and bromocriptine may help treat substance addictions by normalizing dysregulated dopamine circuits involved in reward pathways and cravings. Controlled trials are examining their effectiveness and safety profiles.

The dopamine stabilizing effects of these drugs coupled with psychosocial interventions could potentially rebalance addiction-altered neurochemistry. However, more data is needed regarding risks like medication abuse.

Managing ADHD

Stimulating dopamine activity in the underactive mesocorticolimbic circuits implicated in ADHD is an emerging concept. Some researchers hypothesize gentle dopamine agonists may enhance motivation and impulse control without amphetamine-like overstimulation.

While still highly speculative, selective D2 or D4 agonists could theoretically improve ADHD symptoms like inattention, hyperactivity, and executive dysfunction more smoothly than stimulants. But clinical evidence is still sparse.

The applications reviewed here represent only a sample of the avenues currently being explored with dopamine agonists. As research continues unpacking dopamine's diverse roles in mental health, motor function, hormone regulation, and more, so too will the possibilities for precision drug targeting.

It is an exciting time to be at the frontiers of dopamine agonist development as our understanding of receptor pharmacology matures. The future continues to hold great promise for harnessing and fine-tuning dopamine's gifts therapeutically via designed drug-receptor interactions. With biochemistry leading the way, we edge closer to balanced brain communication.

Calling All Décor Queens: We Need Your Help Spreading Joy!

Now that you've joined me on this uplifting dopamine decor journey, I have just one small request.

In the spirit of spreading positivity far and wide, it would absolutely make my day if you could take just a moment to leave an honest, glowing review about your experience with this book. I know, I know - no one loves asking for reviews. But hear me out!

You see, your thoughtful feedback holds so much power to uplift others. Those few minutes generously sharing your perspective provide a massive lift to this growing design community.

When you post a positive review, you send the mystical book algorithms important signals that these décor tips are truly helping creative spirits like you design happier homes.

This then gives the book more visibility in searches so that others can also stumble upon and benefit from the dopamine decor knowledge you found so helpful. Your review spreads the joy bug.

Plus, your unique perspective, style, and background may give future readers that final nudge of inspiration to take action. Your thoughts can affirm for someone else that these concepts could work wonderfully for them too! Reviews create a sense of relatable community.

Especially for a little indie book just starting out like this one, reviews help immensely. Your support gives the concepts you love "social proof" validity. So if this guide resonated and brought you value, please consider giving it an uplifting boost!

The goal is getting these feel-good, psychology-backed decorating concepts out to as many creative spirits as possible. Your review fuels that dream and lifts my spirits in the process. It's a great feeling knowing my ideas positively impacted someone.

Of course, please share only your honest thoughts - I value your trust and transparency. But if you did gain inspiration from these pages, I hope you'll pass along the gift to others seeking uplifting design advice simply by sharing what resonated most with you.

Sincerely, thank you for even considering. The time you take to spread meaningful ideas matters so much. It allows indie creators like me to keep doing what we love. Now, onward to crafting heartfelt havens!

How Your Review Helps This Book Find Other Like-Minded Spirits

In today's crowded online marketplace, products live or die by reviews. This is especially true for books depending on visibility through Amazon's algorithms and recommendations. Here's a peek behind the curtain at how your ratings help:

Star Ratings Influence Search Results

Books with positive 4-5 star overall ratings rise to the top of relevant keyword searches. Higher stars signal to Amazon the content is resonating. This gives my book visibility when people search terms like "happy home" or "feel good decor." Your stars shine a spotlight.

Glowing Feedback Attracts New Readers

When curious readers scan reviews on a book's Amazon page, glowing testimonials provide that final nudge of assurance. Feedback like "This book changed how I view decorating - it finally feels fun and fulfilling!" convinces readers the content will add value. Your perspective sways hearts.

The More Reviews, the Merrier

A book with just a handful of reviews appears less authoritative at first glance. But hundreds of enthusiastic responses indicate the advice holds widespread worth. The more reviews, the more buzz and social proof. Each adds up!

Beyond Sales: Why Your Review Matters

But here's the thing - this isn't just about numbers or visibility. While that helps sustain my ability to keep creating, what matters most is the people these concepts uplift.

Your review puts dopamine decor on others' radars when they need inspiration most. It reminds them creativity and self-expression matter. You point them toward the joyful path when they're stuck rigidly following "rules."

A simple review plants seeds guiding others home to themselves. And that's really what this is all about - giving courage to decorate boldly from the heart.

So thank you for even considering leaving your impressions. A review may seem small, but its reach is so much bigger than you know. You encourage and connect future readers just by being your wonderful you.

Now, off you go, to craft wonderfully cozy, personal havens brimming with spirit and stories. Please know I appreciate you!

Enhancing Your Reading with Complementary Visuals

While this guide focuses on clearly articulating the philosophies, psychology, and foundational principles behind dopamine decorating through words, I recognize many readers also appreciate accompanying visual examples.

Pictures allow you to vividly envision how these uplifting design concepts might translate into tangible spaces, color palettes, arrangements, and motifs. You conceptualize more fully when absorbing principles both verbally and visually.

That's why I offer access to the Sofia Meri Interior Design Guide. This photo-rich online resource excellently demonstrates visual examples.

With vivid imagery of finished spaces, the duide allows you to illuminated this book in action.

Scan or follow the link below

rebrand.ly/SofiaMeri

Sofia
Meri

About the Author

Following a profound bout of depression, I, as a renowned interior designer, underwent a transformative healing experience, a significant part of which I attribute to the meticulous and intentional redesign of my own bedroom. The walls, now bathed in the optimistic hue of sunshine yellow, became more than just a backdrop; they became a canvas of hope and renewal. Interspersed with cherished family photos, memories of happier times came alive. The room was also adorned with luxuriously cozy textiles, offering tactile solace, and treasured keepsakes that narrated tales of my past. This wasn't just about aesthetic appeal; it was a therapeutic cocoon of warmth, comfort, and inspiration built from the knowledge of my profession.

Each morning, the space I had thoughtfully curated reflected back my resilience, identity, and the enduring beauty of life. The positive symbiosis between my psyche and my surroundings became undeniably palpable. Each corner of my room seemed to emanate a vibrant energy, uplifting my spirits and reinforcing a brighter outlook on life.

With a heart brimming with gratitude and recognizing the power of intentionally designed spaces, I channeled my professional expertise and personal revelations into 'Dopamine Decor.' This book is not just a testament to my journey but an invitation to others to explore the therapeutic potential of their environments. My aspiration is for it to guide others in crafting sanctuaries of joy and solace, showcasing that, even amidst life's tumults, our surroundings can be a balm to our souls. As an acclaimed figure in the world of interior design, my goal is to now fuse emotional well-being with design, sharing this unique blend of joy with the world.

Made in the USA
Las Vegas, NV
26 December 2023

83482256R00090